SEMINAR EDITIONS

SEMINAR EDITIONS

Theodore G. Tappert, General Editor

THE SO-CALLED
HISTORICAL JESUS
AND THE HISTORIC,
BIBLICAL CHRIST

by MARTIN KÄHLER

Translated, edited, and with an Introduction by CARL E. BRAATEN
Foreword by PAUL J. TILLICH

FORTRESS PRESS • PHILADELPHIA

SEMINAR EDITIONS

Christian literature of the past, when read and pondered after the lapse of generations, often sheds new light on the discussion of important questions in our day. Revival of interest in the writings of such diverse figures of the past as Søren Kierkegaard, Blaise Pascal, John Wesley, John Calvin, Martin Luther, Thomas Aquinas, and Augustine (to mention only a few) has served such a function.

Acquaintance with the literature of the past also provides first-hand glimpses into the life and thought of Christians in earlier ages. Men whose names have been encountered in history text-books take on flesh and blood, and important movements in the history of the church come into clearer focus when the literary deposit of other times is read.

It is the purpose of the present series to make available to the modern reader a number of works which deserve to be better known. Most of them are here translated into English for the first time; the few which were originally written in English have long been out of print. All have been edited with care and furnished with introductions and annotations which will help the reader understand them in their historical context.

The choice of various types of literature—diaries, memoirs, and correspondence as well as theological essays—should add interest to instruction for the general reader as well as the student of church history and the history of Christian thought. The same may be said for the inclusion of European as well as American works.

To My Father and Mother

CONTENTS

ix

FOREWORD

As one of the few surviving pupils of Martin Kähler I want to express first of all my joy in the fact that a kind of Kähler revival is taking place. Kähler's prophetic book on the historical Jesus and the Christ of faith anticipates some of the most urgent problems in present day theology. The present edition prepared by Dr. Carl Braaten makes this abundantly clear.

I want to add a few words about the impression Kähler's personality made upon those of us who studied under him in the first decade of this century. He was an imposing figure, powerful in face and in thought, an heir of the classical period of Goethe and Schelling, a convert of the German revival in the 'thirties and 'forties of the nineteenth century, a fighter against the liberal theology which slowly conquered most of the theological chairs at the German universities. At the same time he was aware of the problems produced by the developments in philosophy and by historical research into biblical literature. Kähler was a strictly systematic thinker who developed his ideas under the principle of the Reformers—"justification through faith by grace"—without repeating the traditional formulations of Protestant Orthodoxy.

There are two things which have made Kähler important to a host of pupils, including myself. One was his profound insight into the problem of the historical Jesus in the light of the scholarly research into the sources. This is the subject of the present book. But there was another element in his thought which was even more important for several of my friends and myself, namely, his application of the principle of the Reformation to the situation of modern man between faith and doubt. He taught us that he who doubts any statement of the Bible and the creed can nevertheless be accepted by God and can combine the certainty of acceptance with the actuality of even radical doubt. This idea made it possible for many of us to become or remain Christian theologians.

I do not believe that Kähler's answer to the question of the historical Jesus is sufficient for our situation today, especially in view of the problem of demythologization and the ensuing discussions. But I do believe that one emphasis in Kähler's answer is decisive for our present situation, namely, the necessity to make the certainty of faith independent of the unavoidable incertitudes of historical research. Finding the way in which this can be done for our time is one of the main tasks of contemporary theology. The presentation of Kähler's thought to English readers will be a great help in this task.

PAUL J. TILLICH

University of Chicago
January, 1964

ACKNOWLEDGMENTS

To Paul Tillich I owe the original idea to write my doctoral dissertation for Harvard University on Martin Kähler's theology and to translate this book on the historical Jesus into English. More than that, however, I am indebted to my former teacher for numerous intangible elements of theological study—interest, outlook, and purpose. I am grateful to him for taking the time from his busy schedule to honor the memory of his own former teacher by writing the foreword to this book.

Among the friends who shared the agonies of a beginner in German in his attempts to make Kähler speak English, I wish to make special mention of William Robert Jenson, my lively discussion partner in Heidelberg. He checked my translation for errors and often discovered a better phrase to render a difficult passage. An additional source of help came unexpectedly from the Reverend Henry A. Kennedy, a parish minister in Scotland. Upon hearing that my work on Kähler was ready for publication, he graciously mailed me a translation he had made of Kähler's little book at the suggestion of Professor Thomas F. Torrance. This afforded me the opportunity of comparing the two translations and of benefiting from his efforts. I am happy that now I can acknowledge his thoughtfulness and generosity. To Professor Ernst Kähler, Greifswald, I am grateful for the elucidation of several passages and for the identification of several obscure references.

Finally, it would be an offense against the purest human love on earth to fail to acknowledge the assistance of my wife, LaVonne, to whose lot fell the tedious task of typing the several versions of this work on their way to this edition.   C. E. B.

REVELATION, HISTORY, AND FAITH
IN MARTIN KÄHLER[1]

Carl E. Braaten

The Kähler Renaissance

Martin Kähler (1835-1912) has become again a living voice in contemporary German theology. The three epoch-making theological publications of the twentieth century, namely, Albert Schweitzer's *The Quest of the Historical Jesus* (1906), Karl Barth's *The Epistle to the Romans* (1918), and Rudolf Bultmann's *New Testament and Mythology* (1941), have elaborated motifs which were essential to Martin Kähler's theology. The controversies raised by these three writings have forced theologians to examine the roots of these motifs in the history of theology. In so doing it was inevitable that Martin Kähler would be rediscovered and assigned the place of significance he deserves. Many of the key concepts of the above-named works were anticipated by Kähler. The currents set in motion by Schweitzer's history of the Life-of-Jesus movement, Barth's theology of the Word, and

[1] This Introduction draws heavily on chapters in the present editor's unpublished doctoral dissertation, "Christ, Faith, and History: An Inquiry into the Meaning of Martin Kähler's Distinction Between the Historical Jesus and the Biblical Christ" (Harvard University, 1959). A supplementary essay by the editor, entitled "Martin Kähler on the Historic, Biblical Christ," is available in *The Historical Jesus and the Kerygmatic Christ*, trans. and ed. Carl E. Braaten and Roy A. Harrisville (Nashville: Abingdon, 1964), pp. 79-105.

Bultmann's kerygma Christology now give Kähler's theology a ring of contemporaneity lacking in the great "school" theologies of the nineteenth century which overshadowed Kähler in his day. Kähler moved in—and out of—the theological schools of Tübingen (F. C. Baur) and Erlangen (J. C. K. von Hofmann); he was influenced by Hegelians and Ritschlians but refused to join their ranks. In a very general way he was counted among the biblicists and pietists, yet he rejected verbal inspiration and recoiled from pietistic subjectivism.

No doubt the present renaissance of Kähler's thought is being facilitated because his theological independence has kept him from falling under the same clouds of criticism which dialectical theology caused to hover over the great nineteenth-century systems. The Barthian attack upon the Schleiermacher-Ritschl-Herrmann line of modern Protestantism touched only peripheral elements in Kähler's theology.

The attempts to take the full measure of Kähler's thought have been frustrated by the fact that with apparently equal justification he can be viewed as a forerunner of either Karl Barth or Rudolf Bultmann. Yet, today these two theologians represent opposite extremities of the theological spectrum. Between the two World Wars a number of essays and dissertations tried to establish the degree to which Kähler deserves the blame or the credit for the rise of dialectical theology. Opponents of dialectical theology proposed a return to Martin Kähler as a way of restoring the correlation between a christocentric biblical theology and the life-situation of modern man. It was felt that dialectical theology did not do justice to the cultural, anthropological pole of theology. Still others praised Martin Kähler as the voice in the wilderness of liberalism announcing the ultimate breakthrough in the form of "Crisis" theology. However, after the Second World War the results of Form Criticism and the call to demythologize the New Testament invited theologians to shift their attention from the question of the discontinuity between God and man, the eternal and the temporal, to the question of the discontinuity between history and the kerygma, the Jesus of history and the Christ of faith. Bultmann and his followers have occasionally appealed to Martin Kähler as support for their characteristic theses concerning the relation between faith and the kerygma and between factual history (*Historie*) and existential history (*Geschichte*).[2] A group of Lutheran theologians responded by denying the Bultmannians the right to appeal to Martin Kähler.[3] Martin Kähler is thus drawn into the controversy which still rages between Bultmann's supporters and his antagonists.

There is a growing bibliography of titles dealing with the ambiguous connections between Kähler's theology and contemporary viewpoints.[4] Scholars are asking: Where does Kähler really stand? What did he really say? He can hardly be the father of all those who are called his children. Or could he? And if so, how? Before we view Kähler in modern perspectives, however, it would be well to delineate the general context of Kähler's theological development and examine his response to it.

A Biographical Sketch

Martin Kähler was born the son of a pastor in the year 1835 in Neuhausen near Königsberg, just over one hundred years after

[2] Cf. Hans-Werner Bartsch, "The Present State of the Debate," *Kerygma and Myth*, II, trans. Reginald H. Fuller (London: SPCK, 1962). Bartsch's discussion of Martin Kähler's use of the terms "kerygma" and "history" is from a one-sided, Bultmannian orientation.

[3] Cf. Paul Althaus, *Fact and Faith in the Kerygma of Today*, trans. David Cairns (Philadelphia: Muhlenberg, 1959). The chapter entitled "Martin Kähler and Kerygma Christology" attempts to show how Kähler's theses have been amplified in a distorted way by Bultmann. Cf. also the chapters by the Lutheran theologians Kinder, Künneth, and Ellwein in *Kerygma and History*, ed. and trans. Carl E. Braaten and Roy A. Harrisville (Nashville: Abingdon, 1962).

[4] The best recent study of Kähler's theology is that by Heinrich Leipold, *Offenbarung und Geschichte als Problem des Verstehens* (Gütersloh: Gütersloher Verlagshaus, 1962), which also contains a helpful but incomplete bibliography of works by and about Kähler.

the birth of Königsberg's most famous resident, Immanuel Kant. During his youth the poetry of Goethe and Schiller cast a spell over him. He could appreciate little else. Culturally his roots were deeply imbedded in the Goethe epoch of classical German Idealism, more in its poetic and philosophic aspects than in its artistic. Nature never seemed to stir him much, and music he met with a deaf ear. Of his student days he once said: "I swallowed down Spinoza and read Kant, Schelling, and Hegel."[5] The cast of his mind was of a serious nature; he strove to apprehend ultimate depths, to discern what is universally true and valid, and to find a synthetic unity within the multiple diversities of experience. Even though the course of his intellectual life was to take a theological rather than a philosophical direction, he always retained the philosopher's love for ultimate reality, universal validity, and absolute certainty.

Kähler entered the university to study jurisprudence, but transferred to the theological faculty on the occasion of a serious illness. During his illness Kähler realized that he had not gained from the romantic poets and humanistic culture a firm basis for the assurance of eternal life. He found instead that Paul Gerhardt's hymns meant much more to him in this crisis, when the spectre of death hovered over his bed. They lifted his soul to the worship of the living God manifest in the Christ from whom the poets had shied away. Even after turning to theology, however, Kähler always retained his earlier devotion to Goethe—which explains his unceasing preoccupation with the modern cultured mind enthralled in the Goethe cult. Kähler once said: "Modern men eat more crumbs from Goethe's table than they realize."[6] Kähler's matured theological mind discerned in what he called "the Goethe cult" a relapse into heathenism. For according to Kähler the innermost essence of heathenism is pantheism, the deification of the

[5] Quoted by F. Spemann, "Zur Lebensarbeit Martin Kählers," *Die Furche* (1918), p. 330.
[6] *Ibid.*, p. 329.

created, indeed, the worship of the creature. In Goethe he found no unambiguous confession of God the Creator of heaven and earth. Kähler's answer to the Goethe cult—an answer filled with the apologetic passion of one who himself had shared the love of ethical and aesthetic pantheism—came in 1894 in the form of an impassioned address to the younger generation entitled "The Living God: Questions and Answers, Heart to Heart."[7]

Kähler studied theology in the universities of Heidelberg, Tübingen, and Halle. Heidelberg's systematic theologian, Richard Rothe (1813-85), exercised a decisive influence on Kähler through his lectures on the life of Jesus, on speculative theology, and on ethics. It was also Rothe who introduced Kähler to the New Testament studies of the Tübingen school headed by Ferdinand Christian Baur. Of this experience Kähler said, "This critical cold water bath was the beginning of my own serious studies."[8] The lectures on the "Life of Jesus" planted a seed in Kähler's mind which bore fruit years later in his wholesale rejection of the quest for the historical Jesus. Kähler's dogmatic reflections at this time centered on the doctrine of creation. Wrestling within the context of Rothe's theosophical speculations, Kähler discovered that the diacritical point in the Christian doctrine of creation entailed the rejection of emanationism and, hence, pantheism. Kähler's ultimate solution to this problem took the form of a rigorous distinction between a biblical doctrine of creation and the cosmogonic speculations of theosophy.

At the University of Halle Kähler came into contact with two leading "mediating" theologians, Julius Müller and August

[7] *Der lebendige Gott: Fragen und Antworten von Herz zu Herz* (Leipzig: A. Deichert, 1894).

[8] *Theologe und Christ. Erinnerungen und Bekenntnisse von Martin Kähler,* ed. Anna Kähler (Berlin: Furche-Verlag, 1926), p. 89. The first part of this book contains Kähler's autobiography covering the years 1835-67, written while he was still a young man. The second part, covering the years from 1867 to his death in 1912, is by his daughter, Anna Kähler. The appendices include Kähler's poems, aphorisms, maxims, letters, and a lengthy bibliography of his writings.

Tholuck. Here he encountered a revival of the theology of the Reformation and of Pietism which had rediscovered the religious power in the doctrines of sin and grace, justification through faith alone, and the vicarious atonement. It should be pointed out, however, that the term "mediating theology" (*Vermittlungstheologie*) is used to describe not a homogeneous school of thought, but rather a method of correlating the doctrinal tradition of confessional Christianity with modern scientific thought and methodology. Therefore, while there was a vast assortment of "mediating" theologians, theologically they were generally to be found between a repristinating orthodoxy and an innovating liberalism. In the area of biblical criticism the "mediating" theologians had a conservative tendency, and thus came to be known as "positive" critics in distinction from the "negative" critics of the Bible. As "positive" critics they sought to defend the reliability of traditional views of the Bible on purely literary and historical grounds. Unlike the orthodox Lutherans and the extreme biblicists, however, they ventured to accomplish this rescue operation without recourse to the obsolete theory of verbal inspiration. Kähler also came to be known as a "mediating" theologian, but he frequently had greater affinities with the viewpoints of the "negative" than with those of the "positive" critics.

When Kähler went to Tübingen to continue his theological studies, he found that the classes of the famed Baur were shrinking as a result of the remarkable popularity of Johann Tobias Beck. Beck won over scores of students, who were fascinated by his ability to confront them directly with the biblical message without overburdening it with innumerable fragments of literary and historical information. Kähler later admitted that to Beck he owed in large measure his love for the Bible and his basic confidence in its revelatory contents. Yet, he could not follow Beck's "biblical realism" because it avoided critical problems by escaping into a "pneumatic" exegesis. Of his experience under Beck he said,

"It was too late for Rothe, Müller, and Tholuck to be blotted out of my heart and head."[9]

This brief sketch of the formation of Kähler's theological thought would be incomplete without mention of J. C. K. von Hofmann. Ever since he had read Hofmann's *Schriftbeweis*,[10] Kähler had intended to move on to Erlangen to sit at the feet of the master. However, the urge to complete his dissertation under Tholuck on the biblical idea of conscience persuaded him to return immediately to Halle. Moreover, he felt he had reached the saturation point as a student listening to the lectures of others, and he was restless for an academic post of his own where he would be free to develop his own thought. Thereafter, except for three years as *Privatdozent* (instructor) in Bonn (1864-67), Martin Kähler spent the rest of his days as a professor of systematic theology at the University of Halle. He died in 1912 at the age of seventy-seven, leaving the appropriate request that there be inscribed on his tombstone the *articulus stantis et cadentis ecclesiae,* the evangelical article on justification which had formed the center of his theological system as well as of his faith and life.

Kähler was a prolific writer, beginning his literary career at the age of thirty with the publication of his dissertation on the idea of conscience. The most complete bibliography[11] of his writings lists 165 titles, most of which are timely responses to controversial questions of his day. But by all odds the most balanced presentation of his thought is his *Die Wissenschaft der christlichen Lehre*

[9] *Ibid.,* p. 170.

[10] *Der Schriftbeweis* (Nördlingen: C. H. Beck, 1852-55). The only book by von Hofmann available in English is *Interpreting the Bible,* trans. Christian Preus (Minneapolis: Augsburg, 1959), which is a translation of *Biblische Hermeneutik,* a posthumous work edited by W. Volck (Nördlingen: C. H. Beck, 1880).

[11] The bibliography is included as an appendix in Martin Kähler, *Geschichte der protestantischen Dogmatik im 19. Jahrhundert,* ed. Ernst Kähler (Munich: Christian Kaiser Verlag, 1962), pp. 290-307.

("The Science of Christian Doctrine"),[12] perhaps the greatest one volume work of dogmatics to appear between Schleiermacher and Barth. Kähler's theological system was divided into three parts, each of which is unfolded in the light of the governing principle of justification. The first part is called Christian Apologetics and deals with the motivating presuppositions of justifying faith. The second part is Evangelical Dogmatics; it sets forth the basis and contents of justifying faith. In the third part, entitled Theological Ethics, Kähler traces the correspondence between justifying faith and moral responsibility. Karl Barth has observed that "with the possible exception of M. Kähler, no one dared actually to plan and organize Evangelical dogmatics around the doctrine of justification as a centre."[13] Never before had the material principle of Protestantism assumed preponderant significance for theological methodology. Orthodox Lutheranism loyally handed down the doctrine from generation to generation, but it had become only one among many disconnected *loci*. It fared even worse in the Protestant theology of the Enlightenment. In the Erlangen school of Lutheran theology[14] it began to come into its own once again, and in Kähler's *magnum opus* it received an impressive interpretation both in theological depth and methodological breadth. Kähler's central idea now lives on in the form of Paul Tillich's idea of the Protestant principle. In Tillich's own words: "The power of the Protestant principle first became apparent to me in the classes of my theological teacher, Martin Kähler, a man who in his personality and theology combined traditions of Renaissance humanism and German classicism with a profound understanding of the Reformation and with strong elements of the religious awakening of the

<hr>

[12] *Die Wissenschaft der christlichen Lehre, von dem evangelischen Grundartikel aus im Abriss dargestellt* (Leipzig: A. Deichert; 1st ed., 1883; 2nd rev. ed., 1893; 3rd rev. ed., 1905).

[13] Karl Barth, *Church Dogmatics,* trans. G. W. Bromiley (Edinburgh: T. & T. Clark, 1956), IV, 1, 522.

[14] Actually, the Erlangen theology of von Hofmann and von Frank tended to submerge justification in sanctification, and thus evoked Kähler's charge of subjectivism and perfectionism.

middle of the nineteenth century. . . . He was able not only to unite this idea with his own classical education but also to interpret it with great religious power for generations of humanistically educated students. Under his influence a group of advanced students and younger professors developed the new understanding of the Protestant principle in different ways."[15] Tillich himself was one of these students who developed such an understanding. "The step I myself made in these years was the insight that the principle of justification through faith refers not only to the religious-ethical but also to the religious-intellectual life. Not only he who is in sin but also he who is in doubt is justified through faith."[16]

The Invulnerable Basis of Faith

The two essays in this small book,[17] which now appears for the first time in English translation, offer excellent examples of Kähler's involvement in the critical problems of his day. Kähler's reading of the signs of theological crisis can be summarized in two

---

[15] Paul Tillich, *The Protestant Era,* trans. James Luther Adams (Chicago: University of Chicago Press, 1948), pp. xiii-xiv.

[16] *Ibid.,* p. xiv.

[17] The chief essay, from which the book derives its title, was delivered as a lecture to the Wuppertal pastoral conference. It was first published in 1892 under the title *Der sogenannte historische Jesus und der geschichtliche, biblische Christus* (Leipzig: A. Deichert). A second edition, which appeared in 1896 under the same title, included the original essay plus three additional essays. The four essays appeared in the following order. The first essay, entitled *Do Christians Value the Bible Because it Contains Historical Documents?,* was intended as a preface or introduction to the original essay of 1892, which came next under a new title *How Does Christianity Become Certain of its Historic Christ?* Essays three and four were responses to several critics of the original essay, the third essay being directed against Willibald Beyschlag and Otto Ritschl and the fourth against Wilhelm Herrmann. In 1926 the 1896 edition was reproduced photomechanically.

The first modern edition, which appeared in 1953 (ed. Ernst Wolf; Munich: Christian Kaiser Verlag), included only the original essay of 1892. However, the edition of 1956 (reprinted in 1961), also edited by Ernst Wolf, included after the original essay the first essay in the 1896 edition. The present edition (based on the 1896 edition) includes these same two essays and in the same order: (1) *How Does Christianity Become Certain of its Historic Christ?;* (2) *Do Christians Value the Bible Because it Contains Historical Documents?*

interlocking questions, one focused upon the Bible and the other upon Christ. How can the Bible be a trustworthy and normative document of revelation when historical criticism has shattered our confidence in its historical reliability? And how can Jesus Christ be the authentic basis and content of Christian faith when historical science can never attain to indisputably certain knowledge of the historical Jesus? Underlying both of these questions is the existential quest of faith for a sure foundation, for what Kähler called an "invulnerable area" (*sturmfreies Gebiet*). In other words, how can theology explicate the access of faith to a final historical revelation without being imprisoned in a thoroughgoing historical relativism? Kähler tried to find a solution to this problem which had been posed earlier in Gotthold Lessing's famous formula of discontinuity between accidental truths of history and eternal truths of reason. Søren Kierkegaard's faith was also inundated by the flood of historical relativism, as is evident in the question he formulated in *Concluding Unscientific Postscript:* "How can something of a historical nature be decisive for an eternal happiness?"[18] Kähler's life-long struggle with the problem of how faith can be based upon historical facts if the very essence of faith is its relationship to the supra-historical revelation of God was resolved for him in the biblical picture of the historic Christ. The Bible pictures Jesus Christ as the personal unity of supra-historical revelation and historical reality. Here Kähler found what can be termed a "theonomous" answer to the quest for eternal life. Here we have the "invulnerable area" to which faith has access without falling prey to autonomous subjectivism or heteronomous objectivism.

Of course, Kähler's term "the historic, biblical Christ" is no Pandora's box which contains solutions to all problems. It is an expression which points to the center of a wide circle of component elements which derive their reality and significance from their rela-

[18] Søren Kierkegaard, *Concluding Unscientific Postscript,* trans. David F. Swenson (Princeton: Princeton University Press, 1944), p. 86.

tion to the center. That center, the historic Christ of the Scriptures, is not to be divorced from the ever-widening circle of effects which it has created. These effects in turn become essential presuppositions for the *understanding* of the historic, biblical Christ. In speaking of this Christ Kähler always has in mind a series of effects existing in unbroken continuity with each other and with their ultimate point of origin. Among these are the faith of the individual Christian, the proclamation of the gospel, the confession of the church, the testimony of the Spirit, and the presence of the risen Christ in and through these phenomena. There is no access of faith or understanding to Jesus Christ when any of these elements is absent or ignored.

We shall more clearly understand Kähler's portrayal of faith's "invulnerable area" if we mark off his position from those which he rejected as either subjectivistic or objectivistic. We can do this most concisely if we telescope these positions in the light of Kähler's own critique of them.[19] These positions were also seeking an "invulnerable area" which could support man's hope of eternal life within the context of his finite, temporal, and sinful existence.

The Failure of Nineteenth-Century Subjectivism

According to Kähler the distinctive characteristic of subjectivism is the idea of the productivity of faith with respect to revelation. He encountered this idea in three of the great nineteenth-century theologians, Friedrich Schleiermacher, J. C. K. von Hofmann, and Wilhelm Herrmann.

Kähler criticized Schleiermacher, the father of modern theological subjectivism, for dissolving the objectivity of revelation into religious "feeling" by making the latter productive of the cognitive

---

[19] For more detailed interpretations of Kähler's critique of nineteenth-century theologies, cf. Martin Kähler, *Geschichte der protestantischen Dogmatik im 19. Jahrhundert, op. cit.* Cf. also Heinrich Petran, *Die Menschheitsbedeutung Jesu bei Martin Kähler* (Gütersloh: C. Bettelsmann, 1931).

content of revelation. The positive content of the revelation was conceived as a product of "feeling" translated into concepts of the "pious consciousness." Kähler acknowledged that Schleiermacher admirably succeeded in rescuing religion from its bondage to the rationalism and moralism of the Enlightenment, but believed that he failed to distinguish clearly between a "feeling of absolute dependence" and faith in God who revealed himself in the person of Christ. Revelation through the Word becomes impossible in Schleiermacher's system because the Word is always merely an expression of an impersonally experienced revelation. The norm for revelation is then no longer to be found in the revealed content of faith, but only in the intensity of feeling, or the potency of God-consciousness. The consequence of this view of revelation and religion is that the religious subject gives to revelation its specific content. The biblical Christ is then not—as it is for Kähler—the basis and content of a faith which receives, but he is a figure of history in whom a God-consciousness has been raised to the nth power. He is not the unique and indispensable Mediator of man's communion with God. Instead, faith understood as "religious experience" has become its own basis and productive of its own content.

Kähler admitted that this interpretation and criticism of Schleiermacher is based primarily upon the early Schleiermacher of the *Speeches on Religion.* On the other hand, in *The Christian Faith* Schleiermacher's thought advanced to a christocentric position, a fact which Kähler acknowledged as an abiding contribution to Protestant dogmatics. However, although Schleiermacher here placed the Redeemer in the center of his dogmatics, Kähler felt that the true relation between Christ and the Christian was threatened by Schleiermacher's idealistic monism and that his view of Christ was seriously infected by Marcionism.[20]

[20] Kähler called Schleiermacher a Marcionite because the Old Testament possessed no constitutive significance for Schleiermacher's understanding of the Christian faith.

Related to Schleiermacher's subjectivism of "religious" experience was von Hofmann's subjectivism of specifically "Christian" experience, the experience of the regenerate and sanctified believer. Kähler credited Hofmann with breaking through Schleiermacher's monistic immanentalism by recovering the *Heilsgeschichte* motif of Bengel's school. Thus Hofmann was able to take the concept of historical revelation seriously; yet Hofmann did not escape the limitations of subjectivism. For Hofmann the primary object of theology is the Christian who has experienced conversion. The real source of dogmatics is the new man in Christ. Biblical history and church doctrine come in for consideration only subsequently, that is, to confirm what the Christian theologian as Christian derives from his own experience. The facts of redemption are thus established first as data of faith, and secondly as historical data by detailed research. The great drama of redemptive history is re-enacted in the inner life of the reborn man who by historical research discovers a harmonious parallelism between outer history and internal experience. This "Christian" subjectivism is modified, however, by the fact that the individual believer opens himself to correction by the broader experience of the universal church and the biblical records.

Kähler objected to this pattern of thought because it allows the life of the church and of the individual believer to be relatively independent sources of revelation alongside the Scriptures, and because a measure of productivity is conceded to the religious consciousness as such. Hofmann did demand biblical proofs of the historical objectivity of the content of faith, but these were a mere supplement to a faith which begins by relying upon itself, upon the fact of its own existence. In this way faith is not brought into immediate relation to the historic, biblical Christ, for faith's awareness of this Christ is preceded by an *a priori* awareness of itself. Thus Hofmann could say: "There is nothing more immediate than the fact that I am a Christian. That is more immediate than the fact that I am a man." Or: "I as a Christian am the object of knowledge for myself as a theologian."[21]

Kähler's stubborn refusal to accept the idea that faith is productive of its own content is best illustrated in his polemic against Wilhelm Herrmann's famous distinction between the basis of faith (Jesus) and the content of faith (Christ). Kähler is aware that although Herrmann intended to avoid the subjectivism of the Erlangen school, he did not successfully overcome it. Herrmann's intention was to discover a basis of faith which was neither dependent upon the results of historical science nor invisible to the person who does not yet believe. This supporting basis of faith is "the inner life of Jesus." The man in search of God is led to trust in God on the basis of his vision of "the inner life of Jesus." When he believes, his faith produces, quite spontaneously, specific thoughts which form its content. The divinity of Christ, the doctrine of the Trinity, and the resurrection of Jesus are such "thoughts of faith" (*Glaubensgedanken*). They are examples of faith's experiential interpretation of "the inner life of Jesus" as the sign of the overwhelming love of the invisible God. All references to the miraculous and the supernatural are thoughts of faith, for they transcend what is visible and knowable by natural perception.

Now Kähler turns with all decisiveness against Herrmann's separation of the historical Jesus (the basis of faith) from the biblical Christ (the content of faith). For Kähler the Jesus of history is not a small fragment of the total biblical Christ; instead, the biblical Christ is the historic Jesus. To support this assertion Kähler argues that what is historic (*geschichtlich*) cannot be reduced to what is visible apart from and prior to faith. Furthermore, not even "the inner life of Jesus" can be assumed to be indubitably visible as reality apart from faith, especially since an essential ele-

---

[21] These quotations are from Karl Barth, *Die protestantische Theologie im 19. Jahrhundert* (Zurich: Evangelischer Verlag, 1952), pp. 555-56. Unfortunately, Barth's chapter on von Hofmann is one of the many omitted in the English translation of this volume.

ment in Herrmann's idea of "the inner life of Jesus" is Jesus' messianic self-consciousness. First of all, the question whether Jesus understood himself as the Messiah is disputed among scholars, and, secondly, his claim to be the Messiah could just as easily be evidence of his madness. So Kähler concluded that the inner life of Jesus or his self-understanding cannot be scientifically demonstrated as supra-historical in content or as religiously valid.

The crux of Kähler's objection to Herrmann lies in the latter's interpretation of the resurrection. Kähler could not follow Herrmann in defining the resurrection as a "thought of faith" (*Glaubensgedanke*). The resurrection of Jesus is the ground of faith, a structural element of its basis. Otherwise, faith in the risen Christ is in reality faith in that which has been produced by faith. The correlation between the resurrection-event and the resurrection-faith is collapsed into a subjective identity of faith and its content. On this point we can observe a parallel between the arguments Kähler advances against Herrmann's position and those which some theologians today voice against Bultmann's view of the resurrection. The point is simply this: When the apostles proclaimed the resurrection event, was the primal datum of their preaching something which had happened to Jesus, or was it something which had happened to themselves? Kähler argued that, of course, both belong together. The Easter event included the confessional response to it. Something happened also to the witnesses of the risen Christ, but only on the basis of that which had first happened to Jesus. The history of Jesus Christ includes the event of his resurrection.

The Essence of Objectivism

If the Schleiermacher-Hofmann-Herrmann theological lineage failed to provide an "invulnerable area" for faith and to guarantee faith's access to God's revelation in the historic, biblical Christ, the various objectivistic attempts were, in Kähler's opinion, no more successful. The essence of objectivism is the quest for objective supports upon which the relation between the believer and Christ may be predicated. Hofmann and Herrmann tried to overcome Schleiermacher's subjectivism by various kinds of appeal to objectively given facts. Hofmann required detailed historical and exegetical proofs corroborating the facts read off the consciousness of the regenerate man. Herrmann needed only one objective support, namely, the undeniable fact of the "inner life of Jesus." But Kähler's attack upon the way of objectivism was not directed against Hofmann and Herrmann. Kähler thought of them primarily as representatives of theological subjectivism. On the other hand, when Kähler spoke of objectivism he had in mind Roman Catholicism, Protestant Orthodoxy, and modern historicism. As different as these three phenomena are in many respects, they are united by their common opposition to subjectivism, namely, a spiritualistic-mystic concept of the productive potencies of faith. Such a tendency, they agree, makes the Bible and communal traditions merely reflexes of a subjectivity drawing inferences about itself. Kähler shared the concern of objectivism by refusing to let faith be its own point of support. The question of the assurance of faith, however, is not answered by constructing a system of objective guarantees which a person must accept *in toto* either as a pre-condition or as a co-determinant of faith. All three forms of objectivism in effect harness the Holy Spirit in a dogmatic or historical system.

In Roman Catholic dogmatics the access to the revelation of God in Christ is guaranteed by a massive bulwark of objective supports. The authority of the Roman magisterium, grounded in apostolic succession and papal infallibility, vouches for a virtual encyclopedia of metaphysical and historical knowledge to which a person must assent. Knowledge of the existence of God and of the historicity of Jesus must be reached by reason prior to the act of faith. Rational proofs and historical evidences are worked out by an understanding in search of faith, rather than by a faith in search of understanding. It was Kähler's interpretation of the doctrine of justification that motivated his criticisms of the Roman Catholic concept of authority and demand for objective assurances. Kähler believed that no possible combination of metaphysics and historiography could establish the objects of faith. Therefore, neither the invisible, living God nor the historic, biblical Christ can be known to a person apart from faith. This also means that natural theology and its various proofs of the existence of God cannot serve as prolegomena to Christian dogmatics.[22]

The matter is somewhat different in Protestant Orthodoxy. At first it attempted to defend the objective authority of the Scriptures via its theory of plenary verbal inspiration by the dictation of the Holy Spirit. Questions arising from historical criticism of the Bible were proscribed *a priori*. Later, Orthodoxism was forced to buttress its formal presupposition by appealing to rational historical induction. This was the case with E. W. Hengstenberg who used historical arguments to support the old theories about the Bible. As a repristination theologian he classified Kähler among the rationalists because Kähler felt compelled by the insights of biblical criticism to abandon the theory of biblical inerrancy. But Kähler's real reason for rejecting the orthodox view of biblical authority was that faith in the God of revelation is made contingent upon intellectual certainty that everything in the Bible is historically accurate. The whole structure crumbles with the removal of one element.

Kähler felt that the orthodox definition of faith involving the sequence of *notitia, assensus,* and *fiducia* led to an intellectualistic regimentation of the *ordo salutis*. Volitional assent to intellectual information about God and Christ was made a prerequisite of saving faith. This information was to be found in the Bible and was

[22] Kähler wrote no essays devoted specifically to criticism of Roman Catholic theology. Yet, one finds numerous critical "asides" scattered throughout his works.

secured by the doctrine of verbal inspiration. This attempt of Protestant Orthodoxy to provide a threshold of objectivity over which a person must pass to enter the household of faith was particularly offensive to Kähler because ultimately it constituted an implicit departure from the Reformation doctrine of justification by grace alone through faith alone in Christ alone.[23]

The Polemic Against Historicism

For Kähler modern historicism represented a particularly faithless form of objectivism. In present-day language it is best known as the quest of the historical Jesus. The intention of this quest was to rediscover the authority of the historical Jesus on religious and ethical matters behind the dogmas of the apostles or to trace out the life and thought of Jesus beneath the quilt of ideas thrown over him by the theology of the early church. At this point it may be profitable to comment at greater length upon the specific context and significance of Kähler's polemical writings on the Life-of-Jesus movement.

Why had Protestant theology since Reimarus (1694-1768), the Wolfenbüttel Fragmentist, summoned all of its critical faculties to reconstruct the personality of Jesus in terms of his psychological development and external history? A very common answer to this question is that theology here finally began to take seriously the full humanity of our Lord. It was reasoned that if Jesus was a real man, one could explain his origin and development, his religious genius and moral sensitivity, his ministry and influence according to the analogy of universally human experience. Kähler agreed that Christian faith does have an essential interest in the

[23] Cf. the fourth essay in the 1896 edition of *Der sogenannte historische Jesus und der geschichtliche, biblische Christus* and Kähler's *Dogmatische Zeitfragen: Zur Bibelfrage* (Leipzig: A. Deichert; 2nd ed., 1907), especially the essays *Unser Streit um die Bibel, Das Offenbarungsansehen der Bibel,* and *Die Bibel, das Buch der Menschheit.*

full humanity of Jesus of Nazareth, so well expressed in Luther's dictum that we can never draw God's Son deep enough into our own flesh. But he could not agree that the Life-of-Jesus movement was merely interested in elaborating the concreteness of the incarnation. The interest of faith in the humanity of Christ cannot be decisively satisfied by the results of psychological or historical research into the life of Jesus. We could hardly take the humanity of Jesus any more seriously than the Gospels themselves, and where the Gospels are silent, why should the biographer fill in the gaps by the unbridled speculations of his imagination? Kähler believed that the confession of the true humanity of Jesus was an immediate datum of apostolic faith in the Word made flesh, and not the product of historical scholarship. This confession perpetuated itself in the actual ongoing preaching of the church, and was well known before the rise of modern critical historiography.

In Kähler's view it was not so much devotion to the Jesus of history as antipathy to the Christ of dogma which constituted the real interest of the Life-of-Jesus movement. At least for many historians the recovery of the historical Jesus provided the dynamite to explode once for all the christological dogma of the ancient creeds. Others contrasted the Jesus of history not only to the Christ of the creeds but also to the apostolic picture of Christ. It was not, however, their demonstration that Jesus was a real man of history which offended Kähler in the modern biographies of Jesus, but rather their hidden ebionitism, their obscuration of the transhuman dimensions of the biblical Christ. It was this conviction which caused Kähler to say: "The historical Jesus of modern authors conceals from us the living Christ. . . . I regard the entire Life-of-Jesus movement as a blind alley."[24]

The living Christ is the Christ proclaimed by the apostles. The Jesus of the Gospels is pictured from the very beginning in "dogmatic" terms. To rescue the allegedly "real" Jesus from those ear-

[24] See below, pp. 43, 46.

liest apostolic dogmatic presentations would necessitate going behind the New Testament portrayal of Jesus Christ. Where would one go (sources) and which rules of procedure (hermeneutics) would one follow in the risky business of reading behind or between the lines of our Gospels? For Kähler there was only one answer. When we go behind the sources we go into ourselves, dip out of our own minds and imaginations, and produce, as it were, a fifth gospel. The result of this process of combining self-exegesis and scriptural eisegesis is the "so-called historical Jesus" which Kähler infamized in the title of his lecture: *Der sogenannte historische Jesus und der geschichtliche, biblische Christus.*

What did Kähler mean by the "historical Jesus"? The ambiguity of the expression calls for a clarification of its meaning. In most cases Kähler uses the term in a derogatory sense. In English the term is even more ambiguous than in German, for German theology has become accustomed to a technical distinction between *historisch* and *geschichtlich*, a distinction which Kähler certainly helped to create.

It is well known that considerable offense has been taken at Paul Tillich's statements about the irrelevance of the "historical Jesus" for Christian faith and theology. Yet, those who criticize Tillich should at least be reminded that the theological background for this distinction is not to be sought primarily in the Hegelian contrast between the "Jesus of history" and the "Idea of Christ" but rather in the opposition between *der historische Jesus* and *der geschichtliche Christus* in Kähler's theology. When we analyze the nature of this opposition, we must not expect to find in Kähler's writings the strict terminological purism of modern existentialist theology. Kähler did not always abide by an exclusive categorical distinction between *historisch* and *geschichtlich*. Nevertheless, we can make a few summary observations.

The "historical Jesus" is not the earthly Jesus as such, but rather Jesus insofar as he can be made the object of historical-critical research. The term has primary reference to the problem of historical knowledge, and does not intend to deny or devalue the historicity of revelation. If the "historical Jesus" is fashioned by a method which strives to divest itself of all presuppositions, and to establish objective facts, whether or not anyone has an existential interest in these facts, we can at least understand why Kähler and others like Bultmann and Tillich speak of the irrelevance of the "historical Jesus" for Christian faith. But the "historic Christ" is not irrelevant. This term refers to Jesus insofar as he is the object of faith, the content of preaching, and confessed by the believing community as Lord, Messiah and Redeemer.

The problem of rendering this distinction between *historisch* and *geschichtlich* into acceptable English has disturbed more than one translator. The contrast between the substantives *Historie* and *Geschichte* has been expressed in the following pairs of terms: objective history and existential history, outer history and inner history, or even writing history and making history. Since Kähler normally uses these words in their adjectival form, we have translated *historisch* as "historical" and *geschichtlich* as "historic."[25] Thereby we are assuming that in ordinary English we sense a difference between a "historical" fact and a "historic" event.[26] A historic event has great significance for the future and is remembered by posterity as determinative in the continuous life of people. A historical fact may be completely insignificant to anyone and reg-

[25] The terms "objective history" and "existential history" are used by John Macquarrie in *An Existentialist Theology* (New York: Macmillan, 1955) and the terms "outer history" and "inner history" are used by H. Richard Niebuhr in *The Meaning of Revelation* (New York: Macmillan, 1941) as translations of *Historie* and *Geschichte*. In the present volume, both in the introduction and in the main text, *geschichtlich* and *historisch* have been translated by "historic" and "historical" respectively. In doing so we are following the practice of Reginald H. Fuller in *Kerygma and Myth*, ed. Hans-Werner Bartsch, trans. Reginald H. Fuller (London: SPCK, 1954), pp. xi-xii.

[26] This distinction is noted in the most recent (third) edition of the Merriam-Webster unabridged dictionary. Whereas "historical" usually refers to events or experiences which have taken place in the past, "historic" is usually used to suggest that which is "important, famous, or decisive in history," or as "having considerable importance, significance, or consequence."

istered as a mere disconnected jot in an ancient chronicle. However, the problem which has become acute for modern theology, and was perhaps only partially envisaged by Kähler, is that of defining the relation between these two dimensions of history, particularly when applied to the Gospel accounts of Jesus Christ.

Kähler's attack upon the Life-of-Jesus movement did not mean that he opposed the historical-critical method as such. What he opposed was the false use of this method to write a biography of Jesus or to psychoanalyze him. Kähler was one of the first theologians to question the possibility of using the Gospels as sources for a scientific biography—fourteen years before Albert Schweitzer independently demonstrated the failure of the quest of the historical Jesus. Kähler viewed the matter more radically than Schweitzer, however, and was certainly more skeptical of the historical reliability of the Gospels, at least so far as a biography of Jesus was concerned. But while historically unreliable in the strict scientific sense, the Gospels may still present a trustworthy picture of the Savior for believers.

Kähler entered the debate on the historical Jesus to rectify the boundaries between historical and theological categories, and to show that when scholars switch categories, a great confusion is brought about. The historian too often begins by claiming that he conducts his research purely objectively, without presuppositions, and ends by surreptitiously introducing a set of presuppositions whose roots lie deeply embedded in an anti-Christian *Weltanschauung*. This was happening in Kähler's generation of scholarship. Because this resulted in unclarity and uncertainty in the relation of Christian faith to the biblical Christ, Kähler mounted a powerful offensive against every kind of historicism—negative, positive, and speculative. The "negative" scholars decomposed biblical history into mythology; they operated with the mythological hypothesis of the left-wing Hegelians. The "positive" critics tried to establish the maximal authenticity of biblical history as the basis for living Christianity. The "speculative" historians looked to history for confirmation of their *a priori* philosophy of history. Each of these approaches produced a picture of Christ which Kähler believed conflicted with the biblical picture of Christ. One was offered either a mythic Christ, a moral Christ, or an ideal Christ; Jesus was interpreted as the founder of a historical religion or as the prototype of a religious ideal. Kähler believed that none of these expressions, nor all of them together, captures what the Scriptures, historic Christianity, and personal faith have apprehended in Jesus Christ. Therefore, Kähler used a variety of arguments to demonstrate the illegitimacy of the purely historical treatment of Jesus Christ.

The Christ of the Gospels

First of all, the sources themselves, the Gospels, do not provide us with historical documents (*historische Urkunden*) which can be used to write a scientifically valid biography of Jesus. Nor do they lend themselves to a psychologizing exhibition of the development of Jesus' messianic consciousness. Caustically Kähler described psychological analysis of Jesus' life as being as impotent as soap bubbles. The sources themselves do not contain anything to support the psychologizing rhetoric of the biographies of Jesus. Clearly anticipating the results of Wrede's and Schweitzer's critical studies, Kähler emphatically asserted that the Gospel tradition discloses nothing of a psychological development of Jesus to the time of his public ministry. To assert such a development, the historian has to go behind the sources, read between the lines, and foist upon the texts a principle of organization derived from a modern mood. The modern world-view is retrojected into the mind of Jesus; then historical and psychological analysts are amazed to discover such contemporary relevance in the ideas of Jesus.

Kähler had a totally different view of the purpose of the Gospels. He called the Gospels "passion narratives with extended introductions," a judgment which has proved itself particularly productive and tenacious in the later approach of Form Criticism to the New Testament. The whole New Testament, including the Gospels, he said, is a collection of writings which report primarily the preaching which founded the church. In them we have the preaching of the apostles, the oldest form of Christian preaching, a fact which is historically more certain than that Jesus of Nazareth ever lived. In this preaching all the stress is laid on the cross and resurrection of Jesus as interpreted in the light of Pentecost. Every testimony to Jesus that we possess has been written and preserved from the perspective of the apostles' encounter with him as the risen Lord. Thus, Kähler concluded, we have received from the apostles not a history of Jesus but a portrait of Jesus as Christ and Redeemer, a picture which embraces inseparably both historical and supra-historical dimensions. To ignore the supra-historical dimensions only invites textual chaos. The elimination of the "kerygmatic-dogmatic" texture of the whole in order to ferret out the purely historical elements results in an incoherent scattering of scraps of tradition, which the historian then pieces together under the control of a modern dogma. Some modern dogma or pre-judgment is used in lieu of the apostolic dogma to supply the principle of coherence and reunification.

Kähler's rejection of the Life-of-Jesus movement was supported, as we have shown, by literary and historical insights into the nature of the Gospels. But he also had specifically christological reasons for the rejection. The hidden Christology in the "lives of Jesus" was Arian or Ebionitic. Jesus was pictured as semi-divine or as merely human. Adolf von Harnack's thesis in *What is Christianity?* that "the Gospel, as Jesus proclaimed it, has to do with the Father only and not with the Son"[27] represents the opinion of

---

[27] Adolf von Harnack, *What is Christianity?*, trans. Thomas Bailey Saunders (Harper Torchbooks, 1957), p. 144; italicized in the original.

most of the biographers. Kähler argued that if this is really the case, then not only classical but also liberal Christianity has been committing idolatry. Traditional Christianity worshiped Jesus as God and liberal Christianity worships him as a hero. Liberal Christianity does so without theological justification, for it has replaced Christology with a Jesuanism. Its piety is a case of hero-worship.[28] Kähler was decidedly on the side of the classical doctrine of the divinity of Christ, not necessarily confining the doctrine to the Chalcedonian or Byzantine formulae, but understanding it as a way of expressing the legitimacy of faith in Jesus Christ, without defying the first commandment, without deifying a mere man, and without denying the sinner's need for a Savior.

The basic principle which must be assumed in a biographical or psychological presentation of Jesus is the principle of analogy. Kähler argued that the application of this principle contradicts the New Testament concept of the sinlessness of Jesus. The true humanity of Jesus means that the *form* and *structure* of his life are like ours; but the sinlessness of his humanity means that the *content* and *elements* of his life are also unlike ours. The principle of analogy would work only if both the *form* and the *content* of his life were qualitatively identical with those of universally sinful humanity. So Kähler said: "Sinlessness is not merely a negative concept. The inner development of a sinless person is as inconceivable to us as life on the Sandwich Islands is to a Laplander."[29] There is an insurmountable barrier between Christ and us. That the Savior is *wholly* like us is true; that he is not *only* like us is equally true. If the historian, nonetheless, chooses to

---

[28] Kähler addressed himself to the problems which Harnack's book raised for a christocentric theology of revelation in a series of essays bearing very suggestive titles: *Does Jesus Belong in the Gospel?, Hero-worship and Faith in Jesus, The Confession of the Divinity of Christ* (in Kähler's *Dogmatische Zeitfragen: Angewandte Dogmen;* 2nd ed. [Leipzig: A. Deichert, 1908], II). Harnack's idea that we do justice to Jesus' personal religion when we worship the Father *with* Jesus and not *through* Jesus became the focal point of Kähler's criticism.

[29] See below, p. 53.

disregard this paradoxical assertion, he will not only contradict the unanimous testimony of the sources, but will also create a picture of Jesus inconsistent with Christian faith. He will create a picture of Jesus both pseudo-scientific and void of existential significance. Such a Jesus bears neither the reality nor the power to answer the radical soteriological needs of sinful mankind.

Faith and Historical Science

Kähler undergirded his historico-scientific and exegetico-dogmatic arguments with still another kind of argumentation. He was moved by a deep apologetic concern to preserve the Christian laity from the papacy of scholarship. If faith is made dependent upon the methods or results of historical scholarship, then the historian becomes the priest of Protestantism. To equate the results of research with the facts of faith implies that the believer is dependent upon the oscillating opinions of historians. Faith is made to rest upon a great uncertainty, and in relation to Christ the learned man is given a place of privilege over the ordinary Christian. Thus Kähler said frequently that the special task of the dogmatician as the defense attorney for faith was to make faith independent of false authorities. Therefore, both dogmatism and historicism had to be deposed from their pontificating chairs, for they transmute faith into belief in authorities (*Autoritätsglauben*). They are both "isms" which commit the idolatry of absolutizing dogma or history.

By taking such a stand Kähler was accused by Willibald Beyschlag[30] of committing an outrage against the historical method; and Otto Ritschl, the son of Albrecht Ritschl, charged him with depreciating the results of historical criticism.[31] Ernst Troeltsch

---

[30] Willibald Beyschlag, *Das Leben Jesu* (3rd ed.; Halle: Verlag von Eugen Strien, 1893). The preface to this edition contains a criticism of Kähler's lecture, which had appeared the year before.

[31] Otto Ritschl, "Der historische Christus, der christliche Glaube und die theologische Wissenschaft," *Zeitschrift für Theologie und Kirche*, III (1893), 371-426.

said that "it is merely a figure of speech when one says that simple faith cannot be made dependent upon scholars and professors."[32] His point was that if Jesus is a historical fact, he is, like all historical facts, inescapably subject to the methods of historical research, and faith's estimate of him must wait upon the results of historical science. Such a position is as clearly opposed to Martin Kähler's as it is possible to conceive.

It would be a mistake, however, to interpret Kähler's alleged disparagement of the results of research as an acute case of historical skepticism. The superficial symptoms of skepticism were certainly evident to many of Kähler's critics, but Kähler's deeper motive was to defend faith against every attempt to demonstrate the reality of revelation. What is at stake for Kähler is ultimately the actuality and accessibility of God's revelation in Jesus Christ. Whatever else it may do, the historical method can neither prove the actuality of revelation nor create a mode of access to it. Beyond these two qualifications, it was never Kähler's intention to dispute the validity of the historical method. He had a high regard for it; he saw this method as a gift of providence to the church.

Otto Ritschl argued against Kähler that the only way to secure the historicity of revelation and to verify the biblical picture of Christ was through a historico-scientific demonstration of an authentic minimum of reliable facts concerning Jesus of Nazareth. Only in this way could theology gain an invulnerable foundation for Christian faith and simultaneously one which the Christian apologist could share with the unbeliever for the purpose of awakening faith in him. Kähler answered Ritschl by stating that esoteric knowledge, however so firmly established by science, has no power to awaken and sustain a living faith. The work of historical science requires a special aptitude and technical skills which

---

[32] Ernst Troeltsch, *Die Bedeutung der Geschichtlichkeit Jesus für den Glauben* (Tübingen: J. C. B. Mohr, 1929), p. 34.

the masses of people lack. How then would the unskilled layman gain access to the Jesus of history? He would be forced to choose between conflicting scholarly opinions or to accept on authority someone else's judgments. For even among scholars there is no minimum of wholly assured facts. Historical science is like "a never-ending screw," Kähler said. The assured facts of one generation are disputed by the next. We can never reach beyond provisional validity and probability. Furthermore, the quest for contemporaneity with the Jesus of history leads us at best toward an approximation of the situation which prevailed among the eyewitnesses of Jesus. Yet how infinitely remote they were from faith in Jesus as the Christ of God! How much closer to faith, then, would we be brought by an established minimum of reliable facts? However, Kähler could not regard even this concept of the "minimum" as a valid starting point for securing the foundation of Christian faith.

To my knowledge Kähler is the first Protestant theologian to develop a theological methodology out of the Reformation doctrine of justification through faith alone. Kähler restored this doctrine to a position of dogmatic centrality and drew out its implications for theological method. It was from this standpoint that he entered into conflict with the various subjectivistic and objectivistic approaches which we have described. Against subjectivism his primary objection was that it tended to turn the content of faith into the product of faith. Therefore, the biblical Christ was reduced in breadth and depth to conform to changing subjective criteria. Against objectivism his primary objection was that it substituted alien authorities to serve as the basis of faith, whether the hierarchy in Romanism, the creeds of orthodoxy, the inerrant book of biblicism, or the scientific results of historicism. Therefore, the access of faith to the biblical Christ was obstructed by a detrimental dependence upon intervening authorities. In this light we can understand Kähler's insistence that the biblical Christ is both the basis of faith and the content of faith. He is the revelation of God and the means of access to that revelation. In the communion of the Christian with God, the biblical Christ is the "invulnerable area" from which faith can gain its certainty without relying on the heteronomous guarantees of external authorities.

Kähler was not by nature polemical. He entered into a controversy with great reluctance, and when he did, he seldom mentioned the names of those whose position he attacked. This accounts for the high level of abstraction which characterizes his style of writing. It also, however, confirms his statement that his polemics were intended merely to serve the purpose of a true description of faith's knowledge of God's revelation in the biblical Christ.

The Christological Authority of the Bible

Was Kähler deluded in thinking that believers find an invulnerable basis of their faith in the historic, biblical Christ? This question is of course for the reader to answer after he has fully grasped what Kähler means by the expression. Kähler has other ways of expressing the same idea. He speaks equally often of the living Christ of faith, of the Christ who is preached and believed, of the real Christ who lives in the kerygma and in the hearts of believers. The real presence of Christ is actualized without the support of objective authorities or the midwifery of historical scholarship. This means that there is no genuine knowledge of Christ which is not the knowledge of faith. This faith is utterly dependent upon grace as a miraculous event. Faith and its receptivity in relation to Christ cannot be derived from possibilities immanent in the human situation. Where faith is absent, history is not a pervious medium of the supra-historical reality of the living Christ. Where faith is present, its basis in the historic Christ is confessed, however problematic the historical stuff of that basis may always remain for scientific research.

The living Christ is present to the believer as the Christ who is preached by the church. The kerygmatic Christ lives in the confessional context of the community gathered together by the power of his presence. This contemporary community exists in continuity with its apostolic foundation. Its apostolic foundation is the preaching which founded the church. This preaching itself is the means of the self-manifestation of Christ—the biblical Christ. The biblical Christ, however, is not pictured as an abstract idea, a celestial hero, or a transcendent mythical figure. The biblical Christ is the historic Christ. He is wholly in history, but not merely of history. The historic Christ is not reducible to certain biographical or psychological outlines of the historical Jesus. Faith rests upon the total picture of the total biblical Christ. The total picture creates a total impression of Christ's reality and meaning even though details in the picture are questionable from the standpoint of historical science and comparative religions. The total biblical picture of Christ definitely claims to grasp and portray the saving significance of the man Jesus, and therefore the assurance of the historicity of Jesus is given as an essential element of the faith created through Christian preaching.

Kähler's view of the Bible may also be discussed in connection with the expression, "the biblical Christ." The Christian's relation to the Bible is determined by his relation to Christ. It is because of Christ that the Bible belongs in a class of its own among the great books of mankind. Wilhelm Herrmann, a leading Ritschlian theologian, had stated that the Bible could be interpreted from three different standpoints: as a book of authoritative doctrines, as a book of edifying devotions, and as a book of historical sources. Kähler answered that not one of these perspectives truly grasps what the reality of the Bible has meant in Christian history. Surely the Bible meant more than that to the Reformers and to every evangelical Christian since the Reformation. They viewed the Bible as the proclamation of a message, as the kerygma, Kähler said, which God has given to his heralds and ambassadors. The Bible is nothing less than the Word of God to those who believe in Christ. The experience of the church testifies that this book witnesses to a word of revelation which creates and preserves, judges and renews her whole life. Therefore, the church has acted responsibly when it has acknowledged, on account of Christ, the Scriptures of the Old and New Testaments as the permanent written form of God's revelation, as the critical criterion of church instruction, and as the sources of preaching which awakens faith. The rabbinic and Orthodoxist theory of verbal inspiration does not give us a higher but a lower view of Scripture, because it reverses the relation of Christ to Scripture. It gives us a self-centered rather than a Christ-centered book. It imposes on believers a juridical concept of the Bible's authority. The authority of the Bible should be thought of instead as a creative *authority*, that is, as instrumental in *authoring* faith.

With Kähler's christological view of biblical authority it was possible to arbitrate the painfully fruitless discussion about whether everything in the Bible or only parts of it are the Word of God. The first alternative can be set aside by a *reductio ad absurdum.* The second leads to an interminable controversy about precisely which words in the Bible are to be called the Word of God. There are passages which state what God or Jesus said. Do only these passages, the red-lettered passages of some Bibles, give us direct access to the Word of God? But who is in the position to draw the line between the Word of God and the words of men in the Bible? Kähler preferred a holistic view of the matter. He stated that "the whole Bible is God's Word," keeping in mind the epistemological presupposition of this statement, namely, the union of faith with the living Christ of the Bible. Apart from faith it is meaningless and apart from Christ idolatrous to call the Bible the Word of God.

Kähler's theology of the Word cannot be divorced from his

theology of historical revelation. The reason for this is that the biblical word is the place where revelation, history, and faith meet. The Word of God does not encounter man as a universal truth of reason essentially dissociable from the historical situation in which it was delivered. The word does not come directly from above, unconditioned by its refraction through the prism of history. The Word instead interprets the meaning and value of historical facts. Thus arises the trialogue between revelation, history, and faith. Revelation is the union of an act of God and a word of God. God acts in history and through historical facts. But facts are dumb in themselves. They require a word of interpretation. "Facts become revelation only to a person who understands them as acts of God, and therefore only through the word of interpretation."[33] But it is equally important to Kähler that the accompanying word of interpretation itself be understood as an act of God, for the announcement of the revelatory significance of history is not made by the fortuitous judgment of the religious individual or community. At this point Kähler took issue with Albrecht Ritschl's concept of value judgments (*Werturteile*), for this concept led to arbitrary distinctions between the original facts of revelation and the later interpretations of faith. Herrmann resorted to this idea in his distinction between the historical Jesus as the basis of faith and the biblical Christ as the content of faith, and its latest version may be Rudolf Bultmann's disjunction of the primitive kerygma from the later theology of the church (*Gemeindetheologie*).

Kähler and Modern Theology

Modern theology is showing a new interest in Kähler not only because he brought the question of the inter-connections between revelation, history, and faith into such a sharp focus but also because he so powerfully shaped the terms in which the discussion

[33] Martin Kähler, *Dogmatische Zeitfragen: Zur Bibelfrage, op. cit.,* p. 188.

is being carried on today. A further stimulus to this awakened interest in Kähler's theology is the fact that his influence cuts across such varied theologies as those of Tillich, Barth, Brunner, and Bultmann. It is still too early to assess the extent of his influence on the younger theological generation. However, it is worth noting that this book has enjoyed six editions or printings in the German language, three of them in the past ten years. In addition to this a previously unpublished transcript of Kähler's lectures on the history of Protestant dogmatics in the nineteenth century, edited by his grandson Ernst Kähler, appeared in 1962.[34] Students who can read German will find this monograph a useful and illuminating introduction to the development of German theology in the last century.

Perhaps we ought to add a word of caution against a tendency to overemphasize Kähler's influence on current theology. Kähler has been interpreted as the father of Form Criticism. This has left the impression that one can find the results of this type of analysis in Kähler's writings on the New Testament. What is Kähler's relation to the method of Form Criticism? Kähler himself was not a form critic. There is a world of difference between his method of New Testament study and that of the form critics. Kähler did not "take a particular saying or narrative out of its present context, isolate it, and consider it in reference to its class or type."[35] It was not on this level of detailed technical analysis and classification of Gospel traditions into literary forms that we see a resemblance between Kähler and the form critics. But Kähler did share some of the basic assumptions underlying this method without which Form Criticism could never have been launched and concretely applied. There is no evidence to indicate that the form critics were consciously dependent upon Kähler for their basic assumptions. Erich Fascher, who has written the history of Form

[34] See note 11.
[35] R. H. Lightfoot, *History and Interpretation in the Gospels* (New York: Harper, 1935), p. 31.

Criticism,[36] does not even mention Kähler's name when enumerating the precursors of the movement. He also says that the basic assumptions were a part of the theological atmosphere when suddenly five scholars[37] spontaneously and independently of one another analyzed the synoptic materials in terms of Form Criticism. It is most probable that there was no direct genetic connection between the form critical method and Kähler's evaluation of the Gospel sources. However, we can observe certain generic identities of judgment common to Kähler and the form critics. Thus there may be a small grain of truth in referring to Kähler as the father—at least the stepfather—of Form Criticism.

Very briefly we may in summary fashion mark out the broad areas of agreement between Kähler and the form critics in the tradition of Martin Dibelius and Rudolf Bultmann. They agree that the Gospels are not historical sources which can be used to compose a biography of Jesus. There is no scientific basis for the "Marcan prejudice," namely, the idea that we can take for granted that the narrative framework of Mark is the most historically reliable. The difference between the Synoptics and the Fourth Gospel is one of degree rather than one of kind. Kähler and the form critics agree that the nineteenth-century biographies of Jesus are largely products of the authors' imagination, psychological conjecture, intuited supposition, and novelistic phantasy. Instead, the Gospels are to be viewed as documentary sources which reflect the early preaching which founded the church. Throughout they present the witness of the primitive community to Jesus as the Christ. It is impossible and unnecessary to return behind the kerygmatic witness to a purely historical Jesus, as theological liberalism tried to do. The tradition of Jesus is inseparable from the church, for the Gospels are proclamations by believers of the crucified Mes-

---

[36] Erich Fascher, *Die formgeschichtliche Methode* (Giessen: Alfred Töpelmann, 1924).

[37] Martin Dibelius, Rudolf Bultmann, M. Albertz, G. Bertram, and Karl Ludwig Schmidt.

siah. The preaching and instruction of the community form the life-situation out of which all the recollections of Jesus have been shaped. Every fragment of the Gospel tradition should be interpreted kerygmatically, that is, in terms of its intention. Hence the resurrection event or the faith in the risen Lord becomes the decisive hermeneutical key for New Testament interpretation. Most of these insights have acquired nearly axiomatic significance in current New Testament theology, even among those who do not know Kähler and who are not generally classified as form critics.

The shadow of Kähler lengthens as we turn our attention to the field of systematic theology. The dialectical theologians were no doubt chiefly influenced by Søren Kierkegaard, but for their solution to the problem of historical revelation and faith they were equally indebted to Martin Kähler. All of the dialectical theologians were accused of reacting against the historicistic method so violently that they showed more interest in the dogmatic Christ than in the historical Jesus.[38] However, from the standpoint of the problem which Kähler radicalized, the charge of dogmatic monophysitism (i.e., not taking the historical Jesus seriously) brought against the dialectical theologians results from a misunderstanding. With some warrant one can speak of a methodological monophysitism in Kähler and dialectical theology if this means only that the historical method cannot objectively demonstrate the revelation upon which faith stands.

The dialectical theologians accepted Kähler's definition of the alternatives which theology faces with respect to the problem of faith and historical revelation. Either faith and theology receive the Jesus of history through the tradition of apostolic preaching, namely, the kerygmatic Christ of the primitive community; or the historian must resume the quest of the historical Jesus, by going

---

[38] Examples of this criticism of dialectical theology, otherwise referred to as neo-orthodoxy, may be found in Donald Baillie, *God Was In Christ* (New York: Scribner's, 1955), and George Hendry, *Gospel of the Incarnation* (Philadelphia: Westminster, 1958).

behind the post-Easter witness of the church. The dialectical theologians, if we may use this term elastically enough to include Barth, Brunner, Tillich, and Bultmann, refused to establish faith in Christ by historical inquiry or to look for historical legitimation of the apostolic kerygma. Just as Kähler created an offense by allying himself now and then with the so-called negative biblical critics, so also the dialectical theologians disturbed many conservatives by giving up the battle for biblical Christianity on historical grounds. They could seemingly accommodate the most radical results of the form critics. Indeed, they were roundly accused by many of making a virtue out of a necessity; they seemed to rejoice at every new advance of historical skepticism. If that is true it is not because they wished to remove revelation from history, but because revelation in history simply eludes the grasp of the historian *qua* historian. The category of revelation is not one that the historian with his "profane" scientific method could be expected to take into account. From non-theological perspectives there are no visible traces of revelation in history.

The dialectical theologians carried forward Kähler's judgment that the Life-of-Jesus movement proved itself historically impossible, theologically illegitimate, and apologetically irrelevant. With greater systematic precision and historical sophistication these theologians pronounced the two-century-old search for the historical Jesus a failure and proposed new definitions of the foundation of faith and of faith's means of access to its basis. On the negative side there is widespread agreement between Kähler and the dialectical theologians and also among themselves. On the positive side, however, we find anything but unanimity. This is not surprising in view of the way the dialectical theologians have veered away from each other since those vibrant early days after the First World War. Yet, our common tendency to accentuate the differences between theologians has perhaps caused us to lose sight of their points of common interest. We let ourselves become hypnotized by the crisscrossing of school positions and overlook the abiding bonds of unity.

To a great extent the center of gravity in theology today has shifted from the monumental systems of the dialectical theologians to the short probing essays and monographs of New Testament theologians. The search for the historical Jesus has been renewed, despite the protests of the systematic theologians. The great feeling of emancipation which theologians experienced with the rediscovery of the kerygmatic nature of the New Testament was only temporary. It gave way to an anxiety that the New Testament picture of Christ might be a myth without any real attachment to history. Many have felt that Bultmann's call to demythologize the New Testament might leave us with neither a gospel to preach nor a historical basis of Christianity. Hence, a reaction has set in and the attempt is made to penetrate behind the kerygma to the underlying historical facts[39] or to discover the nucleus of genuine history within the kerygma.[40]

Ernst Käsemann was the first of Bultmann's disciples to call for a resumption of the quest for the historical Jesus. In arriving at a methodological justification of the new attempt Käsemann says that criticism will finally have to turn upon Kähler's book *The So-called Historical Jesus and the Historic, Biblical Christ.* Even after sixty years this book "has not lost its relevance and despite all the attacks made upon it and the many reservations that one may have concerning it, it has also never been really refuted. Basically Bultmann has only given, in his own way, support and preciseness to the theses of this book."[41] Käsemann has correctly

[39] Cf., e.g., Ethelbert Stauffer, *Jesus and His Story,* trans. Richard and Clara Winston (New York: Knopf, 1960).

[40] Cf., e.g., Günther Bornkamm, *Jesus of Nazareth,* trans. Irene and Fraser McLuskey (New York: Harper, 1960).

[41] Ernst Käsemann, "Das Problem des historischen Jesus," *Zeitschrift für Theologie und Kirche,* LI, 1 (1954), 126.

seen that the case for the new quest cannot afford to ignore Käh-ler's attack upon the old quest. The new quest is simply not as new as James Robinson claims in his book *The New Quest of the Historical Jesus.*[42] The major lines of Kähler's criticism have not been rendered obsolete either by new sources or new methods, although the influx of Form Criticism and existentialism are additional factors which have to be taken into account.

We believe that our own situation today parallels in many ways the theological situation in which Kähler produced his book on the historical Jesus. The liberals and the orthodox are fighting their battles on the basis of the always controversial results of historical research; the revelatory foundation of faith is being established by an objectifying science; the essential continuity between the earthly Jesus and the kerygmatic Christ is no longer viewed as a datum of faith but as a debatable historical hypothesis; and withal the assurance of faith is transmuted into a probability of knowledge. Questions of faith are pending the resolutions to questions of fact. The "assured results" of one side are repudiated as fictions of an over-active imagination by the other. One side claims to have new sources (E. Stauffer); another claims to have a new method (J. Robinson), and still another may propose a new Christ. This to and fro of scientific questions is inevitable and desirable, so long as faith is not lured into an attitude of expectant waiting upon what the authorities decide. Then faith has ceased to be living faith and has become mere opinion. It may be that Kähler's little book can strengthen the will of theology to seek first that foundation of faith which not man but God has laid in the biblical Christ, and in doing so to avoid unnecessary detours or inadvisable short cuts.

---

[42] Cf. Van A. Harvey and Schubert M. Ogden, "How New is the 'New Quest of the Historical Jesus'?" in *The Historical Jesus and the Kerygmatic Christ,* trans. and ed. Carl E. Braaten and Roy A. Harrisville (Nashville: Abingdon, 1964), pp. 197-242.

The

SO-CALLED HISTORICAL JESUS

and the

HISTORIC, BIBLICAL CHRIST

*

By Martin Kähler

Doctor and Professor of Theology

*

Second, expanded and revised edition

[INTRODUCTORY REMARKS][1]

Gentlemen and brethren! Some years ago you accorded me your attention when I spoke on the subject of confessing the Spirit of Christ. It will not surprise you that the same person wants to address you today on the subject of confessing the living Christ. For this is indeed my theme, expressed in what seems to me to be a timely antithesis.

The old but ever new question of "Golgotha and Scheblimini"[2] is still very much alive in our own time: "What do you think of the Christ?" (Matt. 22:42). This question is seldom coolly dismissed. Indeed, it elicits a great variety of answers, usually given from the bottom of the heart. But, as you know, the answer given to this question depends, not on what proceeds from our hearts, but on what flesh and blood cannot reveal (Matt. 16:17), what no eye has seen nor ear heard, nor the heart of man conceived, what God has prepared for those who love him (I Cor. 2:9). An

---

[1] All material in brackets has been supplied by the present editor. The supplementing and occasional correcting of bibliographical data has, however, usually not been indicated by brackets.

[2] [An allusion to the work by Johann Georg Hamann (1730-88) entitled *Golgotha und Scheblimini* (1784) which was directed against Moses Mendelssohn's *Jerusalem, oder über religiöse Macht und Judentum* (1783). The Hebrew words *sheb limini* are found in Psalm 110:1 and are translated, "Sit at my right hand." Kähler is not only referring to Hamann's title; he is using the word *Scheblimini* to denote Christ's state of exaltation and the word *Golgotha* for Christ's state of humiliation. In this way he correlates the cross and the resurrection, or the historical and the supra-historical, or the earthly Jesus and the exalted Christ. Kähler, like Hamann, was carrying on a fight on two fronts, against the rationalism of orthodox supernaturalism and the naturalistic rationalism of the Enlightenment.]

answer whose warmth is not matched by its clarity but instead
veils an unclarity is in some circumstances more dangerous than
an outright rejection, particularly for people who are entranced by
the fervor with which the respondent gives his confession.

My theme is a paradox. It places in opposition two statements
which might seem to be saying exactly the same thing. It is intended to counter and clarify what is an ensnaring confusion of
two basically different things. The more difficulty I have had in
achieving clarity at this point, the more intense is my concern to
communicate to others, for their examination, confirmation, or admonition, the insight I think I have attained. And I thank you
for the occasion and opportunity to do so.

I wish to summarize my cry of warning in a form intentionally audacious: *the historical Jesus of modern authors conceals
from us the living Christ.* The Jesus of the "Life-of-Jesus movement"[3] is merely a modern example of human creativity, and not
an iota better than the notorious dogmatic Christ of Byzantine
Christology. One is as far removed from the real Christ as is
the other. In this respect historicism is just as arbitrary, just as
humanly arrogant, just as impertinent and "faithlessly gnostic" as
that dogmatism which in its day was also considered modern.
This judgment applies to both of these as "isms" but not necessarily to those who held, or hold, these erroneous views.

I begin with the question, What is meant by the expression
"historical Jesus"? Like our philosophical terms, it has a history,
and the younger generation has scarcely the slightest notion of

---

[3] [A term Kähler took from Friedrich Nippold's main work, *Handbuch der
neuesten Kirchengeschichte,* III, 1 (3rd rev. ed.; Berlin: Wiegandt and Schotte,
1890), 16. Nippold (1838-1918) was a professor of church history at Heidelberg and Bern. Anglo-Saxons generally know the movement by the title given the
English translation of the first edition (1906) of Albert Schweitzer's history of
the Life-of-Jesus movement: *The Quest of the Historical Jesus* (1910).]

what the term meant in earlier writings.[4] Originally it was used to set the biblical Christ over against the dogmatic Christ. The Son of Man, so life-like and graphic in his words and deeds, the Son of Man as the Gospels portray him and as the Epistles proclaim him, was to step forth from behind that conceptual portrait of Christ which tried to capture in pallid outline[5] the almost irreconcilable features of his unique life. Later the omniscient speculations of Hegel supplanted the dogmatics of Protestant Orthodoxy, substituting the ideal Christ for the dogmatic Christ. Sometime later I. A. Dorner defended the historical Christ against Hermann Schultz, who wanted to leave it to the discretion of each age to produce its own Christ-Ideal, that is, to idealize itself and its own substance in a picture of Christ. The movement gained momentum. Perhaps without really knowing it some fell back upon the course taken by Semler and his colleagues. It seemed that history and dogmatics were both to be found within the Bible: the apostles already believed in Christ when they wrote about him; their witness was therefore already a form of dogmatics. Thus it was supposed that we should have to go behind the preaching of the apostles to their sources in order to find the historical Jesus. And since the fourth evangelist confessed him as the eternal Word, we could expect to find authentic source material only in the so-called Synoptic Gospels. But as soon as it was discovered that even the synoptists were consciously and deliberately *authors,* that in their Gospels pious legends and involuntary distortions had played a part, the only course remaining was to embark on the quest for the historical Jesus who was faintly discernible behind the primitive Christian reports, indeed, behind the original gospel [*Urevangelium*]. This is now being done with great zeal. When we survey the ranks of those engaged in this

---

[4] [Kähler here begins a thumbnail sketch of a long and complex movement of critical research. The best full-length treatment of this movement is still Albert Schweitzer's *The Quest of the Historical Jesus.*]

[5] [Cf. p. 73 below.]

research, we sense in some the loving disposition of a Mary Magdalene, who for all her devotion nonetheless had to be told by Jesus: "Do not touch me!" In viewing the work of others we cannot but feel that although they came out to him with swords and clubs, "passing through the midst of them, he went away."[6] But when he steps among them declaring who he is, who is there who would not collapse in fear and trembling?[7]

My task is then a twofold one: (1) to criticize and reject the wrong aspects of this approach to the life of Jesus and (2) to establish the validity of an alternative approach. The latter is the more important.

[6] [Luke 4:30.]

[7] This last description is unjust if we think of those men who wrote their biographies of Jesus in the tradition beginning with Neander. I thought I had done justice to them in the subsequent paragraphs. Therefore, I am happy to insert a more tempered judgment here. Nevertheless, I must register my conviction that we can only understand the Christ who claims for himself the seat at the right hand of God (Mark 14:62) if we follow the lead of our Gospels and interpret his earthly life from the standpoint of its fulfillment. What people piece together from the Gospels in some other way—supposedly free from embellishments—bears little relation to the Christ before whom generations have humbled themselves. Certainly, portrayals like those of a Renan or a Strauss, which are unfortunately taken seriously even by German theologians, are for believers in Christ an offense which cuts to the quick.

1

AGAINST THE LIFE-OF-JESUS MOVEMENT

{The Impossibility of a Biography of Jesus}

I regard the entire Life-of-Jesus movement as a blind alley. A blind alley usually has something alluring about it, or no one would enter it in the first place. It usually appears to be a section of the right road, or no one would hit upon it at all. In other words, we cannot reject this movement without understanding what is legitimate in it.

The Life-of-Jesus movement is completely in the right insofar as it sets the Bible against an abstract dogmatism. It becomes illegitimate as soon as it begins to rend and dissect the Bible without having acquired a clear understanding of the special nature of the problem and the peculiar significance of Scripture for such understanding. In other cases the problem is simply historical; here that is not so. The justification for the movement can be expressed in Luther's statement that we can never draw God's Son deep enough into our flesh, into our humanity.[1] Every truly evangelical movement shares this point of view in reflecting upon our Savior—ever since John 1 and I John 1:1 ff. were written. But Luther's statement makes sense only if Christ is more than a mere man. It has no meaning at all for those who wish to main-

---

[1] Cited in I. A. Dorner, *Entwicklungsgeschichte der Lehre von der Person Christi* (2nd ed.; Berlin: Gustav Schlawitz, 1853), Part II, p. 544. [Trans. W. D. Simon, *History of the Development of the Doctrine of the Person of Christ* (Edinburgh: T. and T. Clark, 1862).]

tain and demonstrate that he is of no more importance to us than any other significant figure of the past. This was not Luther's view, nor can it be ours, so long as we agree with the apostle that "if you confess with your lips that Jesus is Lord, you will be saved" (Rom. 10:9). If we believe with Christian dogmatics in the Christ who is more than a mere man in his essence, his mission, and his present function—i.e., if we believe in the supra-historical[2] Savior—then the historical Jesus acquires for us that incomparable worth that moves us to confess before the biblical picture[3] of Jesus,

> My soul it shall refresh, my ear
> Can apprehend no tale more dear.[4]

Every detail that we can learn about him becomes precious and meaningful for us. The tradition about him cannot be studied diligently and faithfully enough. Hence a person may immerse himself in Jesus' actions, trying to understand them and to trace them to their presuppositions. So he plumbs the depths of Jesus' consciousness and development before his public ministry; he accompanies the boy Jesus through ravines and fields, from his mother's bosom to his father's workshop and into the synagogue—and then he is most certainly heading up a blind alley!

For the cardinal virtue of genuine historical research is modesty. Modesty is born of knowledge,[5] and he who knows the historical facts and sources acquires modesty in knowledge as well as in understanding. But such modesty is unpopular with many because

---

[2] This is a term coined to designate what, to be sure, would not even exist apart from history but whose significance is not exhausted in the historical effects of a particular link in the chain of history or in the beginnings of a new historical movement, because in the supra-historical what is universally valid is joined to the historical to become an effective presence. Cf. my *Die Wissenschaft der christlichen Lehre* (2nd rev. ed.; Leipzig: A. Deichert, 1893), par. 13. Cf. also pars. 8 f., 365, 397, 404 f.

[3] [The German word *Bild* has been translated as "picture" or "biblical picture," or, occasionally, as "image" or "portrait."]

[4] [From the first stanza of the hymn by Christian Renatus Graf von Zinzendorf (1727-52), *Marter Gottes, Wer kann dein vergessen.*]

[5] [Kähler is punning here on *Bescheidenheit* (modesty) and *Bescheid wissen* (to know).]

their imaginations, sick of the field of speculation, have now pro-
jected themselves onto another field, onto the green pastures of
alleged reality and into the business of historiography by conjecture
or of so-called positive criticism. On this field people are running
wild; they paint images with as much lust for novelty and as
much self-confidence as was ever exhibited in the *a priori* metaphysics of the philosophers or the speculations of the theosophists,
confident (with Richard Rothe)[6] that pious thinking can dissect
God as the anatomist can dissect a frog. As far as the efforts of
positive criticism are concerned, I can very often recognize no difference between the "positive" and the "negative" theologians, to
use the common labels.

To substantiate such a negative verdict some scientific assertions
must now be made which at first sight may seem startling: we do
not possess any sources for a "Life of Jesus" which a historian can
accept as reliable and adequate. I repeat: we have no sources for
a biography of Jesus of Nazareth which measure up to the stand-
ards of contemporary historical science. A trustworthy picture of
the Savior for believers is a very different thing, and of this more
will be said later. Our sources, that is, the Gospels, exist in such
isolation that without them we would know nothing at all about
Jesus, although the time and setting of his life are otherwise entirely clear to historians. He could be taken for a product of the
church's fantasy around the year A.D. 100. Furthermore, these
sources cannot be traced with certainty to eyewitnesses. In addition to this, they tell us only about the shortest and last period of

[6] [Richard Rothe (1799-1867) developed a speculative theological system
uniting faith and knowledge, Christianity and culture. Kähler began his
theological studies under Rothe's guidance and was first stirred to an interest
in the question of the historicity of revelation by his teacher's lectures on the
life of Jesus. Kähler's assessment of Rothe is given on pages 103-18 of the
recently published edition of Kähler's classroom lectures on Protestant theology
in the nineteenth century, *Geschichte der protestantischen Dogmatik im 19.
Jahrhundert,* ed. Ernst Kähler (Munich: Christian Kaiser Verlag, 1962).]

his life. And finally, these sources appear in two basic forms whose variations must—in view of the proximity of the alleged or probable time of origin of these forms—awaken serious doubts about the faithfulness of the recollections.[7] Consequently the "unbiased" critic finds himself confronted by a vast field strewn with the fragments of various traditions.[8] From these fragments he is called upon to conjure up a new shape if his task is to compose, according to modern requirements, a biography of this figure who looms up out of the mist. Even the task of establishing the external course of his life is fraught with serious difficulties—leaving us

[7] This summary will scarcely meet with any serious objection. [In the 1896 edition Kähler added that he was mistaken in this belief—"we are not inclined to draw the final consequences from a view that turns out to be unfavorable to us and to our purposes." He refers the reader to the third essay in the 1896 edition in which he replies to the charges of "morbid skepticism" that had been leveled at him.] The exclusiveness with which we are referred to Christian sources must certainly arouse suspicion outside the Christian circle of vision. The way that the Gospel materials would be handled if we possessed some other sources can be indicated, for example, by the fate of the canonical Acts of the Apostles at the hands of current writers of "histories of New Testament times." In their preoccupation with F. C. Baur and with Strauss's revised edition of his life of Jesus (*Das Leben Jesu für das deutsche Volk*, 1864), people have almost forgotten the earlier edition of Strauss's work, with its interpretation of Jesus' life in terms of myth. But already Strauss's idea is emerging again—very understandably.

The uniqueness of the sources must be evaluated, of course, in accordance with one's view of their general nature. Above all, the relation between the Fourth Gospel and the Synoptics is important for the question of the reliability of the records. I must call attention especially to P. Ewald's work, *Das Hauptproblem der Evangelienfrage* (Leipzig: J. C. Hinrichs, 1890). His reference to the unmistakable one-sidedness of the Synoptic reports (p. 5, cf. pp. 50 ff.) is completely justified. The enigma cannot be solved by passing over the difficulty in silence. In any case, this insight prevents one from pursuing the convenient method of making a bias in favor of the Synoptics into a principle of historical research, and of arbitrarily inserting either a few or many details from the Fourth Gospel into the framework of the Synoptic narrative, or even of borrowing the framework of the Fourth Gospel and then continuing from there as if the presentation of the Synoptics were normative and adequate. Obviously, this essay cannot furnish the specific proofs for these assertions. However, this seems to me unnecessary, for the facts are clearly known and beyond doubt to anyone who has had some kind of theological training. Differences exist only with respect to the evaluation and utilization of these facts.

[8] On the discourses of Jesus cf., e.g., E. Haupt, *Die eschatologischen Aussagen Jesu in den synoptischen Evangelien* (Berlin: Reuther und Reichard, 1895), pp. 5 f.

often with mere probabilities.[9] The biographers, however, set themselves even more difficult tasks. Not all of them refrain from discussing certain questions which titillate one's curiosity but the answers to which still remain irrelevant to the main issue. To cite some examples, there are discussions about how handsome or homely Jesus was, or about his early life at home and at his work. Inquiries into his temperament or his individuality I would put into the same category. We could go on to mention others.

The biographers may refrain from such dubious inquiries, however. The more recent ones, for example, are strong on psychological analysis. They seek to show the variety and sequence of causes that would account for the life and ministry of Jesus. Does the true humanity of Jesus not demand that we understand how he grew, his gradual development as a religious genius, the breakthrough of his moral independence, the dawning and illumination of his messianic consciousness? The sources, however, contain nothing of all that, absolutely nothing! At best only the short story of the twelve-year-old Jesus can pass muster as a historical report; from the standpoint of literary criticism, however, it is sheer caprice to sever it from the infancy narrative of Luke's Gospel. And is there any section of this whole literature that has been treated with more suspicion than precisely this one?[10] To be able to say

[9] We have in mind, for example, the question of the day of the month on which the crucifixion occurred. But even apart from such secondary matters, how meager the prospects of harmonizing just the passion narratives, even when one puts the Fourth Gospel to one side. Of course, if a person assumes the impartiality and objectivity of the records in general, then the questions are not so painful. The materials agree on the whole. It is only the details that we can no longer know. There are many times when historians must accept such restrictions. However, here there is something special to bear in mind that should make one especially cautious. The last week of Jesus' life is the period reported in greatest detail; yet, its actual course impressed itself upon the memory of the eyewitnesses so indefinitely that the later narrators took pains again and again to harmonize the various events and reports—but in vain—and almost each one did it differently from his predecessor. This hardly encourages us to assume such a reliability of the given materials that further conclusions can be drawn with confidence about matters which are not even recorded in the Gospels.

[10] I am, of course, not unaware that it is common for historians to demonstrate from the Gospels the development of Jesus' messianic consciousness during his

anything more about Jesus requires recourse to *a posteriori* conclusions, and to make them cogent calls for extreme caution in one's approach, thoroughly reliable evidence, and a careful appraisal of the significance of one's findings. If we follow this reliable procedure, we shall scarcely achieve lavish results. That this is especially true of the Gospel materials I shall now show through a critique of the current methods used in writing the biographies.

The New Testament presentations were not written for the purpose of describing how Jesus developed. They show him manifesting himself and playing an active role, but not making confessions about his inner life, certainly not unpremeditated ones, except perhaps for a few sighs and ejaculations (e.g., Mark 9:19; John 12:27; Mark 14:36; 15:34).[11] An unprejudiced reader or scholar will hardly deny this. Therefore, the Gospels do not invite the drawing of *a posteriori* conclusions concerning the exact nature of Jesus' earlier development. It is, of course, undeniable that the Old Testament and Hebrew thought-forms have conditioned Jesus' outlook

public ministry. Yet it will surely be generally conceded that such a development is outside the purview of the sources themselves, or of those who reported in them. Therefore, here too the reconstructions are based on what the scholars profess to discover *behind* the sources. I cannot escape the notion, however, that historical research must adhere strictly to the sources. As soon as one disregards the task of evaluating the sources themselves and begins to appraise the materials without paying any attention to their origins and the question of their historicity, one moves merely in the realm of uncertain conjecture. Negative judgments bearing some degree of certainty may be possible; but regarding the actual course of events, one cannot be sure of anything. Otherwise the flawless fiction of a novel would constitute a proof of the reality of its contents. It seems to me that in the work of the critics great unclarity reigns regarding the distinction between psychological (i.e., poetic) truth and the proper reproduction of reality in its often incomprehensible paradoxicality. Whereas present-day artists [*Künstler*] are trying to refrain from purely imaginative effort and pride themselves on faithful reproductions of reality, historians [*die "historische Kunst"*] are pouring their energies into conjuring up before us a past reality from some "psychological law" that seems to be valid for the moment.

[11] Matt. 11:25 f., with its solemn cadence, does not bear the marks of a confession forced out half unwillingly. To me it seems to be a public prayer, like John 17, with conscious reference to the disciples (cf. John 11:41, 42). The other view is supported neither by what follows (verse 28 f.) nor by the context (Luke 10:17-23).

on things.[12] Yet such obvious remarks gain us almost nothing. To assert anything more one must, in view of the silence of the sources, use as a means of research the principle of analogy with other human events—thus contradicting the whole tenor of the Gospel portrayals of Jesus.

First, there is the attempt to use psychology for the purpose of analyzing or supplementing data. Is such an attempt justified in this area? We will admit the validity of psychology only insofar as it rests demonstrably upon experience. A certain trustworthiness may be claimed for it where it deals with the *forms* of our inner experience, and undoubtedly they were the same for Jesus as for the rest of us. But here this is a matter of complete indifference. The dubious studies I have in mind always deal with the *content* of the inner life that developed and manifested itself in Jesus, and with the roots, the development, and the ramifications of his moral and religious consciousness (to use the going terms). Modern scientific psychology, however, no longer busies itself with the content of the inner life. That falls more in the province of other sciences. The poet, too, is accustomed to observe and depict that content. Where does the poet get his information? It is well known that in his poetry Goethe was describing mainly himself and his own experiences. He is such a great man because his observations "penetrated into the depths of human existence." Likewise, sensitive observers are generally impressive painters. Jeremias Gotthelf was as shunned in the region of Berne as Wildermuth was in Swabia—people were afraid of seeing an image of the haunted house in print.[13] Here, too, the person who employs the principle of analogy will have to seek his materials in the mani-

[12] Cf. my essay, *Jesus und das Alte Testament* (2nd ed.; Leipzig: A. Deichert, 1896).

[13] [Under the pseudonym of Jeremias Gotthelf, the Swiss pastor Albert Bizius (1797-1854) penned numerous novels set in the Canton of Berne. Ottilie Wildermuth (1817-77) is known for her narratives of life in Swabia. Both writers' use of clearly recognizable characters and settings in their writings did not endear them to their friends and acquaintances.]

foldness of reality. Therefore I ask once again, Is this method justified in writing about Jesus? Will anyone who has had the impression of being encountered by that unique sinless person, that unique Son of Adam endowed with a vigorous consciousness of God, still venture to use the principle of analogy here once he has thoroughly assessed the situation? We must not think that we can solve the problem with a pantograph, reproducing the general outlines of our own nature but with larger dimensions. The distinction between Jesus Christ and ourselves is not one of degree but of kind. We all know that poets create unreal and impossible figures insofar as they idealize them and cease to portray them with mixed qualities. Such idealization usually means simply the elimination of all the displeasing traits. We cannot, however, deal with Jesus merely by removing the blemishes from our own nature—that would merely leave us with a blank tablet. Sinlessness is not merely a negative concept. The inner development of a sinless person is as inconceivable to us as life on the Sandwich Islands is to a Laplander.[14] In the depths of our being we are different from him, so different in fact that we could become like him only through a new birth, a new creation. How then can we hope to analyze and explain Jesus' development, its stages and changes, in analogy with the common experience of humanity? Indeed, if we look deeper we encounter the objection, How could he have been sinless in the midst of a world, a family, and a people so full of offense? How could the boy Jesus develop in a pure and positive way when in his years of infancy, filial dependence, and immaturity he was surrounded by bad influences, and when his whole education, however well meant, must have been on the whole distorted? All this is a miracle which cannot be explained merely in terms of an innocent disposition. It is con-

[14] With good reason Dorner preferred the expression "sinless perfection," although he too did not think of Jesus as fully developed right from the beginning.

ceivable only because this infant entered upon his earthly existence with a prior endowment quite different from our own, because in all the forms and stages of his inner life an absolutely independent will was expressing itself, because God's grace and truth became incarnate in him. In view of this fact we would all do well to refrain from depicting his inner life by the principle of analogy.

There remains the historical analogy. Here one goes back to the conditions and the thought world of Jesus' environment and to the historical records and Jewish literature which still survive from that period. Perhaps an examination of the history of such attempts will place them in proper perspective. Long before Baur, Semler had discovered the Judaistic tendencies[15] of the early Christian writers. Yet Semler's school exempted Jesus from any such attachment to Judaism. Was this mere prejudice or was it the result of observation, of a correct insight? David Strauss found Hellenistic influences in Jesus, or in any case something totally unrelated to late Judaism. If we compare the Jesus of our Gospels with Saul of Tarsus, we do in fact see a great difference between the disciple of the Pharisees and the Master. On the one hand we see the true Jew, so profoundly and indelibly influenced by the cultural forces of his people and epoch; on the other hand we see the Son of Man, whose person and work convey the impression of one who lived, as it were, in the timeless age of the patriarchs. Thus a return to the first century does not appear to be very promising.

Obviously we would not deny that historical research can help to explain and clarify particular features of Jesus' actions and attitudes as well as many aspects of his teaching. Nor will I exaggerate the issue by casting doubt on the historian's capacity to trace the broad outlines of the historical institutions and forces which influenced the human development of our Lord. But it is

---

[15] [Das "Judenzen," the term Semler used; see M. Kähler, Geschichte der protestantischen Dogmatik im 19. Jahrhundert, op. cit., p. 34.]

common knowledge that all this is wholly insufficient for a biographical work in the modern sense. Such a work is never content with a modest retrospective analysis, for in reconstructing an obscure event in the past it also wishes to convince us that its *a posteriori* conclusions are accurate. The biographical method likes to treat that period in Jesus' life for which we have no sources[16] and in particular seeks to explain the course of his spiritual development during his public ministry. To accomplish that something other than cautious analysis is required. Some outside force must rework the fragments of the tradition. This force is nothing other than the theologian's imagination—an imagination that has been shaped and nourished by the analogy of his own life and of human life in general. If, in other areas, the historian's muse often paints pictures which lack every breath of the past and its distinctive characteristics, what will it make of this unique material? The Gospels confront each of us with an Either/Or. The question is whether the historian will humble himself before the unique sinless Person—the only proper attitude in the presence of the norm of all morality. What a difference it must make in a person's interpretation whether he confesses the sinlessness of the Redeemer whom he is portraying or whether he charges Jesus with a catalog of sins, whether, with Jesus, he reckons every sinner as lost or whether he regards the boundaries as so fluid that moral errors are viewed as exaggerated virtues![17]

It is plainly evident that the imagination which thus orders and shapes the Gospel materials is being guided by still another force,

---

[16] Bernard Weiss, however, does not do this.

[17] Thus Theodor Keim, *Geschichte Jesu* (3rd ed.; 1873) [Zurich: Füssli, 1875], p. 372 [p. 368]. Keim perceives a lack of harmony in the moral development of Jesus at several points. He noticed in Jesus the "scars" of a person refined through conflict, which David Strauss was not able to discover, although Strauss maintained that it was necessary and therefore self-evident to assume "individual perturbations and defects" in Jesus' development. Those who know the literature will recall the disgusting tirades of Renan, for example, in connection with the Gethsemane episode.

namely, by a preconceived view of religious and ethical matters. In other words, the biographer who portrays Jesus is always something of a dogmatician in the derogatory[18] sense of the word. At best he shares the point of view of the dogmatics of the Bible; most modern biographers, however, do so only to a very limited degree. Indeed, quite a few place themselves in conscious opposition to the "primitive world-view of the New Testament."

With this observation, however, we have made a very important discovery. There is no more effective method for securing the gradual triumph of a political party than to write a history of one's country like that of Macaulay.[19] Stripped of its historical dress, the bare thesis of the "historian" would arouse too many suspicions. Disguised as history, the historian's theory passes imperceptibly into our thought and convictions as an authentic piece of reality, as a law emanating therefrom. Thus Rotteck's "history" of the world was in reality a party pamphlet, which, through its wide distribution, shaped the political thinking of large numbers of the German middle class.[20] The same is true of dogmatics. Today everyone is on his guard when a dogma is frankly presented as such. But when Christology appears in the form of a "Life of Jesus," there are not many who will perceive the stage manager behind the scenes, manipulating, according to his own dogmatic script, the fascinating spectacle of a colorful biography. Yet no one can detect the hidden dogmatician so well as a person who is himself a dogmatician, whose job it is to pursue consciously and intentionally the implications of basic ideas in all

[18] Naturally those who think of themselves simply as historians and claim to be completely without bias will view the dogmatician in this way.

[19] [Thomas Babington Macaulay (1800-59), whose *History of England from the Accession of James II* was a best-seller in its day, was politically a Whig and has often been accused of partiality in his treatment of the rise of the Whig party and in his writing of history generally.]

[20] [Karl W. R. von Rotteck (1775-1840) was a leading member of the liberal party and a writer of history. Kähler is here referring to his *Allgemeine Weltgeschichte*, a four-volume world history.]

their specific nuances. Therefore, the dogmatician has the right to set up a warning sign before the allegedly presuppositionless historical research that ceases to do real research and turns instead to a fanciful reshaping of the data.

We all enjoy it when a gifted writer interprets a significant figure or event of the past in a play or novel. By freeing his portrayal from the requirements of historical accuracy and by giving his imagination freer rein, he can sometimes better reveal the true character of the event or figure. In biblically oriented circles, however, epics about the Messiah and dramas about Christ have always been viewed with some uneasiness; and, for the most part, we certainly share these reservations and these qualms. How many authors of the "Lives" blithely compose epics and dramas without being aware that this is what they are doing! And because this is done in prose, perhaps even from the pulpit, people think that this is merely a presentation of the historic, biblical picture of Christ. Far from it! What is usually happening is that the image of Jesus is being refracted through the spirit of these gentlemen themselves. This makes considerably more difference here than in any other field. For here we are dealing with the source from which the outpouring of the purifying Spirit is to proceed now as it has in the past. How can the Spirit perform his purifying work if he is not permitted to reach our ears and hearts without obstruction?

{The Real Christ of Faith and History}

Let us take a good look at this matter. What is the Life-of-Jesus research really searching for? In going behind Jesus Christ as he is portrayed in the church's tradition—and this means also behind the New Testament picture of Christ—it wants to get at the *real* Jesus, as he actually existed in all those respects that all, or some, might consider important or indispensable, or often only desirable or titillating ("How interesting!").[21] Although the attempt to answer concerns such as these encounters the various kinds of difficulties we have pointed out, it is important that we capitalize on the opportunity they offer to seek out the legitimate element in such self-imposed quests. We shall find the answer when we succeed in isolating the real and ultimate reason behind the attempt—legitimate and indeed unavoidable as it is—to present the historic figure of Jesus, in its full reality, to our inner perception.

This brings us to the crux of the matter: *Why* do we seek to know the figure of Jesus? I rather think it is because we believe him when he says, "He who has seen me has seen the Father" (John 14:9), because we see in him the revelation of the invisible God. Now if the Word became flesh in Jesus, which is the revelation, the flesh or the Word?[22] Which is the more important for us, that wherein Jesus is like us, or that wherein he was and is totally different from us? Is it not the latter, namely, that which he offers us, not from our own hearts, but from the heart of the living God? I do not want to be misunderstood. That

---

[21] Even a serious theologian has been known to go astray by speculating on Mary's relation to Jesus on such a matter as his laundry! In the case of Schiller, students try to conclude from his financial state of affairs at a given point in his life—as ascertained from his notebooks—his incentives for public activity or his state of mind. If a theologian lacks a comparable basis for such imaginative additions to the tradition about Jesus, then these embellishments are merely a piece of phantasy, which is the exact counterpart, on another level, to the Moravians' playful intimacy with the Savior. This shows lack of taste even from the aesthetic point of view. For even the keenest aesthetic sensitivity can show a lack of delicacy in treating sacred subjects.

[22] The person well versed in Scripture will not answer that it is the flesh which reveals and the Word which is revealed, for precisely the Word itself is the revelation. Cf. the quotation from Luther, cited by Herrmann [p. 240 in *Der Verkehr des Christen mit Gott* (4th ed.; Stuttgart and Berlin: J. G. Cotta'sche Buchhandlung Nachfolger, 1903), p. 220 in the translation of the 2nd rev. ed. (1892) by J. Sandys Stanyon, *The Communion of the Christian with God* (London: Williams and Norgate, 1895)]: "We must let the humanity of Christ be a way, a sign, a work of God, through which we come to God" (*Erlanger Ausgabe*, 7,73) [*Church Postil, Sermon on Romans 15:4-13* (Second Sunday in Advent); Lenker Edition, VII, 54; *Weimar Ausgabe*, 10^{1,2}, p. 84, lines 26-27].

he was like us is, of course, incomparably significant for us and is treasured by us; Scripture always emphasizes it, too, but hardly ever without adding expressions like "without sin," "by grace," "in humility and perfect obedience," etc. (Heb. 4:15; 7:26, 27; II Cor. 8:9; Phil. 2:6 f.). How he was like us is self-evident. It is also fairly obvious why the evidence of his likeness to us is to be found on every page of the Gospels. And yet how we have to search to muster such a biblical proof from statements which deliberately emphasize that likeness. Does this not explain why we recognize the emphasis on Jesus' moral achievement [*die sittliche Arbeit*] as a distinguishing peculiarity of the Epistle to the Hebrews? (Cf. 2:17, 18; 4:15; 5:7 f., perhaps also 12:2, 3).[23] If a person really asks himself what he is looking for when he reads the Gospels, he will admit to himself, "I am not seeking someone like myself, but rather my opposite, my fulfillment, my Savior." When a person reflects on what he finds when reading the Gospels, he will say, "No man has ever spoken or acted thus; never has such a man existed." He will not say that no one has ever said the same things Jesus said. For Jesus repeated many things which religious thinkers had written and said prior to him—things which become different, however, when he says them.[24] Nor will a reader of the Gospels maintain that everything Jesus did was unique, for he stands surrounded by a cloud of witnesses. And yet, there is something unique in the *way* he did things, for there has never been a man like him.[25]

Why, in the final analysis, do we commune with the Jesus of our Gospels? What does he offer us? "In him we have redemp-

[23] These are passages that emphasize how important his moral achievement is for us, but also that it is important only because it appears striking in the light of his *total* person.

[24] One might compare, for example, the Lord's Prayer with the Jewish prayers which in fact bear a resemblance to it. (See August Tholuck, *Die Bergrede Christi* [5th rev. ed.; Gotha: F. A. Perthes, 1872].) One also ought to note Jesus' use of Scripture. Cf. also the writing by Haupt cited earlier.

[25] On pp. 53 f. we indicated in part what we mean by the "uniqueness" of Jesus. More will be said about this subject toward the end of our discussion.

tion through his blood, the forgiveness of our trespasses"[26] (Eph. 1:7). Do I really need to know more of him than what Paul "delivered to [the Corinthians] as of first importance, what [he] also received, that Christ died for our sins in accordance with the Scriptures, that he was buried, that he was raised on the third day in accordance with the Scriptures, and that he appeared" (I Cor. 15:3 f.)? This is the good news brought in the name of God (I Cor. 15:12 f.; Rom. 1:1 f.; II Cor. 5:18 f.; Gal. 1:6 f.). This is the witness and confession of faith which has overcome the world (I John 5:4). If I have all this I do not need additional information on the precise details of Jesus' life and death.

Then why the Gospels? Why do we need that kind of preaching the content of which is, so often, what Jesus did and taught? We have redemption through *him*.[27] "Who is to condemn? Is it Christ Jesus, who died, yes, who was raised from the dead, who is at the right hand of God, who indeed intercedes for us?" (Rom. 8:34). "We have an advocate with the Father, Jesus Christ the righteous" (I John 2:1). "For we have not a high priest who is unable to sympathize with our weaknesses, but one who in every respect has been tempted as we are, yet without sinning" (Heb. 4:15). We need, we have, and we believe in the living Christ. We believe in him because we know him; we have him as we know him; we know him because he dwelt among us, full of grace and truth, and chose for himself witnesses through whose word we are to believe in him (John 1:13, 14; cf. I John 1:1 f.; John 15:27; 17:20).

Therefore, the reason we commune with the Jesus of our Gos-

---

[26] I adduce this quotation of course only to summarize the answer, not as an adequate proof. That is hardly necessary; the New Testament and the catechisms are clear enough in this respect.

[27] I place this emphasis on these words from Eph. 1:17 [7] and Col. 1:14 in order to bring out the contemporary significance of Christ's *person* for all generations instead of only asserting Christ's work in the past. (Cf. my *Wissenschaft der christlichen Lehre, op. cit.,* pp. 397, 411 f., 432 f.) We are speaking here — as will surely be recognized — not of conversion to Christianity but of the ongoing life of the Christian.

pels is because it is through them that we learn to know that same
Jesus whom, with the eyes of faith and in our prayers, we meet at
the right hand of God, because we know, with Luther, that God
cannot be found except in his beloved Son,[28] because he is God's
revelation to us, or, more accurately and specifically, because he
who once walked on earth and now is exalted is the incarnate
Word of God, the image of the invisible God—because he is for
us God revealed.

That is what the believer seeks. That is what the church cele-
brates.

How important, therefore, the least little feature becomes! How
indispensable the removal of every optical illusion created by the
prism of tradition, the removal of every obscurity in the interpretation of his first witnesses! How inexpressibly important the
reality of Jesus, down to the minutest detail! It would be serious
if this were really the case. Just suppose that the art of modern
historiography were able to carry out a spectral analysis on the
Sun of our salvation. Suppose that we today were able to remove
those obscurities in the tradition. What would that imply with
respect to our fellow Christians in the early period? If their con-
templation and worship of the Jesus of the Gospels were distorted
and deflected by those obscurities which the critic professes to find
in their writings and feels bound to remove, then indeed they
would not have known their Savior. And the same would be true
of all subsequent Christians, including ourselves. Yes, gentlemen
and brethren, what about ourselves? What would our situation be?
Where do we come to know this Jesus? Only a very few can
carry on the work of historical science, and only a few are sufficiently trained to evaluate such work. To be sure, such work would
relieve us of the authority of the Bible, but it would in turn sub-

[28] Theodosius Harnack, *Luthers Theologie* (Erlangen, 1862-86), II, 81 f.;
cf. also *ibid.*, I, 111 f.; Gottfried Thomasius, *Christi Person*, II (2 ed.; Erlangen,
1857), 210 f.; Julius Köstlin, *Luthers Theologie* (Stuttgart, 1863), II, 155,
300 f., 383.

ject us to the authority, not of an empirical science, but of the alleged results produced by this science. Meanwhile there is no one who can answer our question, Where is that fifth evangelist[29] capable of providing us with the picture of the exalted Christ, the picture of God revealed?[30] Which of the biographers can do this? We have our choice in a series from Hess and Zündel, through David Strauss, right up to Renan and Noack, to say nothing of the Social-Democratic pamphlets.[31]

If someone should object at this point, "Our situation with respect to dogmatics is the same as that with respect to historical science, for in relation to dogmatics we are dependent upon theologians," the comparison would be erroneous. Dogmatics is a matter of judging data that are accessible to every Christian, so long as it does not deal with detailed theological propositions that are not really essential in understanding the Christian faith. Historical research, on the other hand, requires the mastery of a sophisticated technique and a massive erudition. In this field no lay judgment is possible, except perhaps the kind made by inflated dilettantes.

Therefore, either we must do without the revealed God, or the reality of Christ as our Savior must be something quite different from the scarcely accessible, or even inaccessible, reality of those

[29] Assuming, that is, that one cannot be satisfied with Renan's fifth gospel, namely, with a geography and ethnography of modern Palestine. [Cf. the introduction to Renan's *Life of Jesus*.]

[30] [At this point Kähler inserted a long footnote replying to the charge by his colleague at Halle, Willibald Beyschlag, that Kähler expected from the biographers of Jesus something they had never claimed to do: "to paint 'a picture of the exalted Christ,' insofar as such a picture is distinct from that of the earthly Jesus" (Beyschlag, *Das Leben Jesu;* 3rd ed., Halle: Strien, 1893; I, xix). "Just the opposite is the heart of my argument," says Kähler. "Otherwise why would I concern myself at all with the biographers? The discussion that follows concerning the preached Christ surely makes that clear. . . . For me, the connection between the earthly and the exalted Christ is expressed in the term 'suprahistorical' (see above, p. 47). . . ."]

[31] [For a description of the place of these biographers in the Life-of-Jesus movement, see Albert Schweitzer, *The Quest of the Historical Jesus.* Some of the pamphlets of the German Social Democratic party in the nineteenth century pitted the socialist teachings of a "proletarian" Jesus against the "bourgeois" Jesus of ecclesiastical Christianity.]

clear and transparent details of his personal life and development which are generally deemed essential in the writing of a modern biography. There must be another way to reach the historic Christ than that of scientific reconstructions which employ source criticism and historical analogy.

Consider for a moment. What is a truly "historic figure," that is, a person who has been influential in molding posterity, as measured by his contribution to history? Is it not the person who originates and bequeaths a permanent influence? He is one of those dynamic individuals who intervene in the course of events. What they are in themselves produces effects, and through these effects their influence persists. In the case of thousands of people whose traces in the history of their contemporaries and of posterity are obliterated slowly or not at all, their earlier development remains for scholarship just so many roots hidden underground, and the particulars of their activity are forever forgotten. The person whom history remembers lives on through his work, to which, in unforgettable words and personal characteristics, a direct impression of his dynamic essence often attaches itself. And the effect left by that impression is necessarily conditioned by the material on which it leaves its mark and by the environment upon which it had to and was able to work.[32] Thus, from a purely historical point of view the truly historic element in any great figure is the discernible personal influence which he exercises upon later generations. But what is the decisive influence that Jesus had upon posterity? According to the Bible and church history it consisted in nothing else but the faith of his disciples, their conviction that in Jesus they had found the conqueror of guilt, sin, temptation, and death. From this one influence all others emanate; it is the

[32] The solitary figures who left only a written legacy, but left no mark on their contemporary world, are not historic figures. Jesus, however, the ministering friend of men, is as different as is conceivable from this sort of "eyeing" of posterity that reckons on being counted among "the class of people that are still to come."

criterion by which all the others stand or fall. This conviction of the disciples is summed up in the single affirmation, "Christ is Lord."

Contemporary history contributed nothing to this affirmation, and Jewish theology still less. The contemporary historical accounts in Josephus mention John, the son of Zechariah, but not a word about Jesus of Nazareth. Indeed, contemporary history counted him among the dead. After he died as a sacrifice for the sake of the nation (John 11:49 f.), the Jews went raving and racing to their political destruction, without taking any notice of him. The small band of Nazarenes was of no importance to them. The rest of the world would have ignored him, had not Saul of Tarsus gathered a community in his name, the giant tree growing out of the mustard seed, under whose leaves the birds of the heaven build their nests. So much for contemporary history.

But what about Jewish theology and eschatology? We surely know how vigorously the unpretentious Rabbi had to contend with the terrestrial hopes for a splendiferous Son of David who was to lay the kingdoms of this world, in all their glory, at the feet of his people. Those images and metaphors from Jewish eschatology which Christians drew upon in painting their vivid pictures of the Christian hope still constitute the stumbling block which is apt to betray the hope of faith into denial of itself.

"Christ is Lord"—this certainty neither flesh nor blood can attain, sustain, or impart. Jesus himself said as much to Peter after his confession (Matt. 16:17), and he said it also in reproach of the unbelieving Jews (John 6:43 f.); it was confirmed by Peter's denial in the outer court of the High Priest and later by Paul, who could say it to his congregations in full expectation of their assent (I Cor. 12:3). Yet, wherever this certainty has arisen and exerted an influence, it has been bound up demonstrably with another conviction—that Jesus is the crucified, risen, and living Lord. And when we ask at what point in their discussions the historians deal with this certainty, we find that they begin not with the much disputed and disconnected final narratives of the evangelists but with the experience of Paul. They ascertain the unwavering faith of the early church as far as they can determine the testimonies and the traces left by those early witnesses. The risen Lord is not the historical Jesus *behind* the Gospels, but the Christ of the apostolic preaching, of the *whole* New Testament. To designate this Lord as "Christ" (Messiah) is to confess his historical mission, or as we say today, his vocation, or as our forefathers said, meaning essentially the same thing, his "threefold office." That is to say, to confess him as Christ is to confess his unique, supra-historical significance for the whole of humanity. Christians became certain that Jesus was the Messiah, the Christ, in total opposition to public opinion, not only with regard to the idea of the Messiah (that is, the way one conceived of the Messiah and what one expected of him), but also with regard to the person of this Jesus of Nazareth. This was as true then as it is today. When Christians tried to make the Messiahship of Jesus credible in their sermons and then in epistles and gospels, they always made use of two kinds of evidence: personal testimony to his resurrection, based on experience, and the witness of the Scriptures. As the living Lord he was for them the Messiah of the Old Covenant.

Therefore we, too, speak of the *historic Christ of the Bible.* It is clear that the historical Jesus, as we see him in his earthly ministry, did not win from his disciples a faith with power to witness to him, but only a very shaky loyalty susceptible to panic and betrayal.[33] It is clear that they were all reborn, with Peter, unto a

---

[33] Jesus' statement in Matthew 16:15 f. does not mean that his person and ministry have produced this confession. Rather, he ascribes this confession to God's revelation. He is not speaking about faith at all; hence, faith is not the "rock." The faith in question had so little power to endure of itself that it needed an explicit prayer to God, whose revelation evoked the confession in the first place (Luke 22:32). The *biblical* Jesus expected that the disciples' witness to him would be with power only after the Spirit had been sent (Luke 24:48 f.; John 15:26; Acts 1:4, 8).

living hope only through the resurrection of Jesus from the dead (I Pet. 1:3) and that they needed the gift of the Spirit to "bring to their remembrance" what Jesus had said, before they were able to understand what he had already given them and to grasp what they had been unable to bear (John 14:26; 16:12, 13). It is clear that they did not later go forth into the world to make Jesus the head of a "school" by propagating his teachings, but to witness to his person and his imperishable significance for every man. If all this is clear and certain, it is equally certain that Jesus' followers were capable of understanding his person and mission, his deeds and his word as the offer of God's grace and faithfulness only after he appeared to them in his state of fulfillment—in which he was himself the fruit and the eternal bearer of his own work of universal and lasting significance, a work (to be exact) whose most difficult and decisive part was the *end* of the historical Jesus. Even though we once knew the Messiah according to the flesh, now we regard him thus no longer (II Cor. 5:16).

This is the first characteristic of Christ's enduring influence, that he evoked faith from his disciples. And the second is that this faith was *confessed*. His promise depends upon such confession (Rom. 10:9-10), as does also the history of Christianity and our own decision of faith. The real Christ, that is, the Christ who has exercised an influence in history, with whom millions have communed in childlike faith, and with whom the great witnesses of faith have been in communion—while striving, apprehending, triumphing, and proclaiming—*this real Christ is the Christ who is preached*. The Christ who is preached, however, is precisely the Christ of faith. He is the Jesus whom the eyes of faith behold at every step he takes and through every syllable he utters—the Jesus whose image we impress upon our minds because we both would and do commune with him, our risen, living Lord. The person of our living Savior, the person of the Word incarnate, of God revealed, gazes upon us from the features of that image which has deeply impressed itself on the memory of his followers—here in bold outlines, there in single strokes—and which was finally disclosed and perfected through the illumination of his Spirit.

This is no reassuring sermon. It is the result of a painstaking consideration of the data at hand. It is the result achieved by a dogmatics[34] which sorts and sifts the evidence and states the conclusions in biblical language only because they happen to agree with the word of Scripture. Ought such a conformity to Scripture really provide a reason for looking with suspicion on this kind of dogmatics, especially among those who base their criticisms on Reformation (!) theology?

In popular usage the word "dogmatics" has come to connote arbitrary assertions, whereas "historical study" of a subject is regarded as always laying hold of reality. The latter is unfortunately not always the case, since historical science does not always observe its limitations or fulfill its obligations, nor is it always in a position to do so. It is equally true that the popular assumption about dogmatics is basically unfounded, though understandable in view of the dogmaticians' aberrations. Dogmatics also has a "given" with which it works, although this is not merely a past reality. Dogmatics is in a very real sense the mediator between past and present; it puts what is genuine and indispensable in the past at the service of the present. This task of mediation, then, belongs to dogmatics, after it has made a thorough and serious study of what historical study can accomplish and has learned from

[34] It is surely plain that I am here contrasting dogmatics with preaching, and scientific statement with untested interpretations. In the context the farthest thing from my mind is the arrogant assertion of the superiority of dogmatics to historical study, or a "tutelage" of historical study by dogmatics. Nevertheless this is the way Dr. Beyschlag interprets my sentence (see his *Leben Jesu,* p. xx); and by putting a colon before the words "This is," rather than indicating that they begin a new paragraph, he leaves readers with the impression that such an assertion was made by me. He also omits everything which makes clear that I am here referring to the portrayal of Jesus in the Gospels, interpreted of course from the viewpoint of the faith one encounters there as well as in the rest of the New Testament.

history what is important enough to warrant consideration by dogmatics. The task of dogmatics is to provide an inventory of our assets.

The "data at hand" to which we referred above are not the individual events reported in the Gospels about the life of Jesus. In this whole discussion we are trying to explain how inadvisable and indeed impossible it is to reach a Christian understanding of Jesus when one deviates from the *total* biblical proclamation about him—his life as well as its significance. The factual data which have led me to this judgment have to do with the nature of the tradition at our disposal. I have in mind especially two far-reaching facts: first, the impossibility of extracting from the sources a "genesis" of Jesus the Messiah and, second, the knowledge of what Christ has always meant to his church and still means to every believer today. These facts are, of course, a distillation of a series of other facts, as I have tried to indicate and as I intend to elaborate more fully. As far as the second is concerned, it is quite unwarranted to demand that the significance of Christ for Christianity be measured by what he means to those whose devotion to Christ has all but ceased. We must remind ourselves again and again that in trying to arrive at an understanding of man we must of course take into account the stages of his development, his existence as a fetus and as an adolescent, as well as his possible degeneration to the level of a cripple or an imbecile; nevertheless our conception of man will, in the last analysis, have to rest on a mature and healthy specimen of noble attributes. We may, if we wish, keep our christological formulae to the barest possible minimum, yet for Christians Christ must always be the object of faith in the "strictly religious sense of the word," to use an expression in vogue today. Otherwise we fall outside the bounds of his church. For this reason Christian language about Christ must always take the form of a confession or a dogma.

Those are the limits of the circle within which I would expect the validity of these arguments to be acknowledged or at least to receive sympathetic consideration.

I can appreciate fully how a person will necessarily reach a totally different position if he denies or depreciates what we have called the second fact. If revelation is only an erroneous name for religious consciousness in its historically conditioned development, and if Jesus is merely a religious genius surpassing the rest of us only in degree, then doubtless the New Testament confession of faith, which also inspired the evangelists in their portrayal of Jesus, can only result in an obscuring of the facts. Then we must look with suspicion on everything, or almost everything, in that portrayal. Then we can only resort to the attempt to explain, at all costs, the mystery of this man in terms of the thought and life of his day, a man who not only wanted to be called the Messiah, but also was confessed and proclaimed as such by an astonishing number of people. Given these presuppositions, I do not look for widespread support of the affirmative side of my criticism. On the other hand, I expect the negative side of my criticism to be generally conceded, so far as it concerns the evaluation of the sources. At any rate, my arguments deal only with those theologians who wish to write a "Life of Jesus" in the service of the confession of Christ, and who think (at least some of them) that their work can do more to strengthen this confession than can dogmatics. I am concerned with a correct evaluation of what the constructive historical method can accomplish, particularly what it can contribute toward the right attitude to Christ within the church, the bearer of the gospel.

The rest of this essay will emphasize why we have the right to be sensitive to, and on guard against, all later embellishments of the biblical picture of Christ. Such imaginative reconstructions cannot stand without criticism, not even as specialized theological research. I think I can explain its popularity and influence in wide circles, especially in the younger generation. Often we do not sufficiently appreciate to what extent the moods regarding the criterion and aim of knowledge change with the times. I say "moods" advisedly. I believe I can observe such a mood at the present time. Historical detail is very much in vogue today, despite widespread skepticism. Historical novels have contributed much to the blurring of the boundaries. Even Christian readers have been spoiled. Instead of approaching the early witnesses sympathetically, searching for the truth in their writings, they prefer to be stimulated and excited by the curiosity of one who was a contemporary, of one who was enflamed into passionate involvement, of one who delighted in the victory of the controversial orator. Although the psychological novel presented in the form of letters may have declined in popularity, we have in its place biographies consisting almost wholly of diaries and fragments of letters. People like to view the remote past in a modern refraction. *Homo sum*—man in every time and place is one and the same, today as always, as is illustrated by the sensation which a short story can create. In spite of these objections one might be able to put up with such attempts in the area of theology if they held themselves in check and heeded admonition. To accommodate a current mood one might conceal his displeasure at such bold manipulations of the noble elements of Jesus' picture.

However, it is another matter when—pardon my bluntness— the Christ-novels ascend to the pulpit. Lengthy discourses about first century history, seemingly profound insights into Jesus' inner life (supported by observations on the differences in outlook between then and now), poetic descriptions of the countryside—all this keeps the listener preoccupied with things which, after all, are merely the vehicles of the events in the Gospels and keeps him from the real thing, or better, from the Person who alone is worthy of our attention, from the one Person in his incomparable uniqueness. Certainly no age should be prevented from speaking its own language and from remaining true to its own character.

However, the restraint and sobriety of the first witnesses should remain the criterion for the message which the evangelical preacher has to deliver. We should attempt to do only *one* thing in our pulpits, namely, to present to our hearers these old, often heard, "outdated" stories—just as they stand, yet freshly and as if heard for the first time. Each listener should receive an indelible impression of what these accounts mean for him. If we immerse ourselves in our Gospels and consider them from every angle without a slavish and lazy adherence to the appointed lessons of the church year, there will be no danger of monotony—unless by monotony one means the repetition of the one keynote, which indeed is unavoidable. This, after all, is the obligation and final aim of every evangelical preacher (Phil. 1:18).

It is a mistaken notion to think that it is enough simply to draw the attention of people to Jesus. The "interest" that is aroused here might easily become an obstacle to genuine attentiveness. That is to say, an interest in antiquity or in a modern psychological interpretation of some well-known event may become an obstacle to a true estimate of Christ's worth for our day. It is as noxious for outsiders as it is for "Christian" circles when Christ and the gospel become mere topics of conversation. A preacher must always be scrutinizing his sermons to see whether he is entertaining his congregation instead of witnessing to the gospel, whether he is engaging their intellect and judgment instead of reinforcing (with appropriate means) their inner stirrings in the direction of radical decision and providing their spiritual life with lasting nourishment. Even under the pretence of promoting biblical knowledge it is possible to do nothing more than "beat the air."

2

THE FOUNDATION OF FAITH
IN THE CHRIST OF THE WHOLE BIBLE

{The Biblical Picture of Christ}

Does this settle the matter? Must we simply accept the statements of the apostles and the New Testament, taking these as the limits of theology, now and henceforth? Is this the way we must always proceed, that we continue to demand and to subscribe an *authoritarian faith* in relation to the Bible in spite of the questions the critics have raised regarding the origin of the biblical writings and the reliability of their statements?

Let us begin with an observation—for me, an observation of decisive significance. The biblical picture of Jesus, the image of his appearance in history, ought to have for us a meaning which transcends a grateful interest in a bygone but mostly misunderstood benefactor of humanity. The question should still be one of faith in Jesus Christ himself. Of course, faith must not be made to depend on what a philosophically trained mind may think about such questions as how God and man are mutually compatible in the inner life of Jesus, how much there was of God in him, how much of man, or how he was at once both wholly God and wholly man. Certainly faith does not depend upon a christological dogma. But it is just as erroneous to make it depend on uncertain statements about an allegedly reliable picture of Jesus that has been torturously extracted by the modern methods of historical research—a product having as little chance of succeeding in the establishing of faith as does the shadowy outline of Christ which dogma has constructed from mere concepts. For in relation to the Christ in whom we may and should believe the most learned theologian must be in no better or worse a position than the simplest Christian. No better, I say, for he comes no nearer to the living Savior than the simple Christian; and no worse, for if his faith has to overcome stumbling blocks, so does that of the simple Christian. For both there exists only one royal way of overcoming these stumbling blocks: "Repent and believe in the gospel" (Mark 1:15)—Jesus Christ died for our sins according to the Scriptures, was buried, and on the third day rose again according to the Scriptures (I Cor. 15:1-5). The only theology whose validity I accept is one which helps to express the facts of a present and living Christianity in the clearest, sharpest, and most adequate way. As the simple scriptural theology of Pietism once deposed the dogmaticians from their papacy of learning, so today it is the task of the dogmatician, in defense of the plain Christian faith, to set limits to the learned pontificating of the historians. They "occupy a larger territory than they can maintain."[1] They undertake to satisfy the demands of a merely scientific curiosity while lacking means adequate to the task; at the same time they fail to observe clearly and decisively the boundary between the concern of the scientific impulse and that of faith in Christ.

Today we often hear that the "Lives of Jesus" have supplanted christological dogma or will have to do so. Then we are presented with a mass, or with an apparent totality, of facts—which must rightly remain subject to endless scholarly inquiry—as incontestable truths of faith or, if one prefers, as incontestable experiences of faith. This is bound to produce an uncertainty, a postponement

---

[1] [Quoted from Matthias Claudius, *Sämmtliche Werke des Wandsbecker Boten* (Gotha: F. A. Perthes, 1882), p. 159.]

of the formation of convictions, a situation of doubt and indecision precisely in the minds of those who go deeper into the matter— all of which assails the root of Christian faith. Since it is evident from such presentations themselves that, in their over-all treatment as well as in their detailed observations, they are merely attempting to lay hold of the past, they must come to terms point by point with other equally diligent and serious efforts.[2] Or, if they do not do this, they achieve the semblance of certainty by temporarily forgetting and suppressing certain data. Yet this deception cannot last for long. If historical research is meant to "lay the foundation"—the one and only foundation[3]—it will soon become clear that such a foundation will provide no real support. For historical facts which first have to be established by science cannot *as such* become experiences of faith. Therefore, Christian faith and a history of Jesus repel each other like oil and water as soon as the magic spell of an enthusiastic and enrapturing description loses its power.

Nevertheless, when we consider the relation of faith to its object, there seems to be no essential difference whether the content of faith derives from the substance of the biblical accounts or from a scientifically produced picture of Jesus. Whichever way we go, the discussion seems to lead ineluctably to the choice between subjectivism and an authoritarian faith which binds us either to the Bible or to contemporary theology. Rather than make ourselves cross-eyed by staring at this choice, let us look away from it for the moment and fix our attention on the position of the ordinary Christian.

Certainly in most cases Christians will have to come to Christ "through" the Bible—not very many through their own reading of it, to be sure; most of them will have been introduced to the

[2] Notice how many things W. Beyschlag and B. Weiss find to discuss in each other's presentations, and how much (or little!) they expect from this for the final result.

[3] [Cf. I Cor. 3:10-11.]

contents of the Bible through sermons or devotional books. The Christian's faith in Christ and his trust in this unique book are inseparably intermeshed in the high esteem in which he has come to hold the Bible. But when it finally comes to making a distinction, it will be clear to the Christian that "we do not believe in Christ for the sake of the Bible but in the Bible for the sake of Christ," as a venerable preacher, well versed in Scripture, once entitled one of his sermons.[4] In the context of our discussion, an even more precise formulation might be: we put our trust in the Bible as the Word of our God for the sake of its Christ.

Lay people who know their Bibles should not be startled by such a statement. The Bible itself tells them as much. What benefit did the Jews derive from all their boasting about the Bible? Knowing Micah did not lead them to Bethlehem to worship (Matt. 2:6). From Scripture they learned that no prophet could arise in Galilee (John 7:41 f.), and so they concluded that nothing good could come out of Nazareth (John 1:46). They did not perceive that the Scriptures bear witness to Jesus (John 5:39 f.), for they understood neither the Scriptures nor the power of God (Matt. 22:29 f.). They stood helpless before the mysteries of biblical prophecy (Matt. 22:41 ff.). Ony those Jews who by faith accepted Jesus as the Christ found their way to the Nazarene (Matt. 2:23), discovered the biblical witness to his Galilean origins (Matt. 4:12-16), and learned by the demonstration of the power of God in the resurrection (Rom. 1:4; II Cor. 13:4) that Moses and all the prophets bore witness to him (Acts 3:18 f. and *passim*). At all events, we learn from this that the way to understand the Scriptures is by going through Christ. Only this "detour" can guard against the danger that loyalty to Scripture may even become a hindrance to faith, as in the case of all unenlightened zeal

---

[4] The sermon, by Dr. Heinrich Hoffmann of Halle, has so far as I know not been published. [Kähler dedicated his dogmatics (*Die Wissenschaft der christlichen Lehre*) to Hoffmann, "my spiritual guide in youth and in manhood."]

for God (Rom. 10:2). We, too, must take this warning to heart, even though our circumstances differ from those of Paul and his contemporaries.[5]

Most of the time we live confidently in our faith without stopping to give an account to ourselves of the roots from which it has sprung. We are first compelled to a retrospective examination when beset by temptations to doubt. The hour for such an examination with regard to the Bible's significance for our faith has struck, and not merely for theologians. Our task, then, is to distinguish cleanly between things which never can or should be separated. We must distinguish between that which is offered to faith and that which motivates faith to grasp what has been offered. It will be true for every evangelical Christian, indeed for every genuine Christian who cleaves with childlike trust to his Savior, that this motivating factor ultimately lies in his experience of surrendering himself to his Savior. Yet the Savior with whom he lives is not someone known only within his own experience or imagination. He is rather the One who is preached to him. He is always—clearly or obscurely, but ultimately—the Christ of the Bible. The more converse a person has with the Bible itself, the more he finds that the drawing power of the Savior merges with the authority of the Bible. Because his Christ is the biblical Christ, and because his realization grows that he has the Bible to thank for his Christ, the Christian comes to believe that he has received not only this Christ but also his faith from the Bible.[6] To no small degree this is because the Bible proclaims Christ, proclaims him from and in faith, and we in turn come to faith through its faith. Yet it is true that no one has an independent faith of the kind and quality attested by the New Testament if he cannot say to the New Testament writers what the Samaritans said to the woman, "It is no longer because of your words that

[5] Cf. my essay *Jesus und das Alte Testament,* Thesis 6.
[6] Cf. my essay *Unser Streit um die Bibel* (Leipzig: Deichert, 1895), pp. 11 f.

we believe" (John 4:42), if he has not been enthralled by the figure of Jesus as was the fourth evangelist (John 20:31; John 1:14, 16), if, by the drawing power and revelation of the Father, he does not believe in the biblical Jesus for the sake of Jesus' word, for the sake of Jesus himself (Matt. 16:17; John 6:44 f., 68; John 20:28 and 14:5-9).

When, as has happened recently, Christian faith is defined as a being "overpowered" by Christ as he encounters us in the picture the Bible paints of him, that seems to me a fitting definition so far as it refers to the finally decisive and sufficient motivating factor in faith and piety.[7] However, I regard the definition as inadequate if it is meant to include also the origin and the mediation of this faith. Also I regard it as too vague so long as this picture itself is not more clearly characterized. For to me the picture which has the effect of "overpowering" us is precisely that of the Christ grasped by faith, the picture of Christ preached from and in faith, and therefore most emphatically not the picture of an extraordinary human being. No, the picture of Christ which has such an effect is that which bears within itself a dogma, a confession of faith, even if what is affirmed were nothing more than a claim to uniqueness. That is to say, this kind of picture presents the figure of the *Lord,* the Savior of the world, the Redeemer from sin and guilt, God revealed. Not only in its content but in so many words, this picture of Christ confronts each person with the Either/Or: cornerstone or rock of offense (I Pet. 2:6-7).

In making a decision when confronted by this picture—whether that decision takes place in scrupulous self-examination or only half-consciously in unreflecting devotion—two impelling forces interact. The one is receptivity, the need to see the deficiency and impotence of one's inner life transformed into self-assurance in the face of one's finitude, and into strength of will in the face of

---

[7] I have particular reference to Wilhelm Herrmann's *Der Verkehr des Christen mit Gott* (2nd ed., 1892).

abhorrent evil. Without this there may be admiration and venera-
tion but certainly not faith capable of sacrificing one's own life
for that of another. The other force is the impression which this
marvelous picture makes upon the receptive beholder. The ordinary reader of the Bible receives this impression in exactly the
same way as does the theologian engaged in research. The difference is merely that the theologian will and must try to define the
content and nature of this impression as clearly as possible and
then explain his reasons. If he is successful he will be rendering
a service to the whole church and, in some instances, to the ordinary reader of the Bible as well, especially should the latter's unreflecting confidence be shaken in one way or another. Let us attempt to sketch briefly the path which lies before the theologian.

The picture of Jesus which confronts us in the Bible is a marvelous one. Doubters have said, not without reason, that even the
Synoptists' portrayal of Jesus is a legend of a saint painted against
a golden background. Yet all the biblical portrayals evoke the undeniable impression of the fullest reality,[8] so that one might venture to predict how he might have acted in this or that situation,
indeed, even what he might have said. This is why to commune
with Jesus one needs nothing more than the biblical presentation.

First of all, we must pause to ask why the impression evoked
by the biblical picture is so strong and overpowering. Do not our
poets create vivid personalities which make unforgettable impressions upon us? Is it not possible that the figure of Jesus is the
loftiest poem of mankind, as some are now saying of an Abra-
ham or a Moses? It is precisely this comparison which advises us

[8] The assertion that in the Fourth Gospel a Logos-automaton is speaking
ought by now to be regarded as obsolete. Far be it from me to deny that this
idea is still circulating and that it will again enjoy greater popularity. The
person who thinks that what is most important is "biographical transparency," or
"conformity to the normal course of events," will hardly receive the impression
mentioned above. What is needed for that is a mind for which external happen-
ings are only signs, a mind inclined to understand a person above all in his
moral and religious aspects and possessing enough modesty and patience to live
with him, so to speak, and to enter into his peculiar style of life.

to the contrary. These personalities may tower more than a head above us, yet they remain flesh of our flesh. If they ever lived, then they were children of men; if they were only invented, then they are children of the imagination, which derives its material from our reality. Carlyle had good reason for speaking of the inexorable truth of the biblical portrayals, for all of these portrayals are of people like ourselves. But what about the biblical picture of Jesus? That it seems so familiar to us now is an understandable delusion. We know this picture from childhood on up, and we live in a society whose best members have received their finest qualities from Jesus and shine with the reflected splendor of his glory. But if we paused to reflect and look around, then he would surely seem very strange to us in his noble sublimity. Yet he seems as lifelike and real as if we had seen him with our own eyes. How could such a realistic picture of the sinless One be a poetic creation?[9] Poetry has only sinful men within its purview, and poetry of whatever kind selects its most vivid subjects from among them. The "unambiguous," idealized characters of drama are justly criticized as unrealistic figures. The biblical picture of Christ, so lifelike and unique beyond imagination, is not a poetic idealization originating in the human mind. The reality of Christ himself has left its ineffaceable impress upon this picture. Were this not so, all the scholars would long ago have ceased to rack their brains over the sphinx-like enigma of this person.[10] Because it is so, thousands have been able to live with him as if he were their most intimate and influential friend.

In continuing with this subject, I do not need to give detailed illustrations and proofs. I am stating, thank God, nothing but well-known facts. Perhaps there is one additional thing I can do,

[9] Cf. above p. 53.

[10] It is very instructive to read over again how David Strauss wrestles with the uniqueness of Christ without its ever occurring to him to lump the biblical portrayal of Christ with the myths (see Strauss's *Das Leben Jesu für das deutsche Volk* [1864], pp. 206 f.).

namely, what every commander does for his courageous troops—
he draws them up to do battle at the strategic point.

Well, then, someone may object, "You speak of a 'picture' of
Jesus. Your 'picture' will also turn out to be an arbitrary figment
of the imagination which the religious thinker has constructed
from the tradition and shaped to suit his purposes. Whenever one
speaks about reality, one looks for what happened in history. The
Gospels, after all, present a narrative, and therefore one must seek
from them a history of Jesus and not a picture of him." But wait—
is this really the case? To be sure, we have narratives, but were
these really preserved and compiled with a view to "pragmatism"?[11] This is certainly not true of the large collections of say-

----

[11] "Pragmatism" [in the writing of history] originally designated [a tracing
of] the causal connection of events. Unlike a "dogmatizing" treatment, it fixes
its attention on the *causae secundae* in the life of Jesus. Recently the "development of his consciousness" has also been stressed. Hence it follows that the
scholar's interest should be directed primarily to the time preceding the Last
Supper. During this period he must observe the development of what thereafter
has only to manifest itself. In contrast to the emphasis of the ancient church on
the "work" of Jesus, now it is his "person" which is supposed to emerge,
precisely in its development. The sayings of Jesus are looked upon more as
"remarks" and "activities" and less as his instruction of the people and of his
followers. All this seems to me to be quite the opposite of the way the figure
of Jesus is actually reflected in the New Testament. To state the matter somewhat provocatively, one could call the Gospels passion narratives with extended
introductions. Mark 8:27 to 9:13, the group of events from Peter's confession
at Caesarea Philippi to the transfiguration on the mountain, shows clearly where
the emphasis lies for the narrator. By the seventh chapter John is up to Jesus'
last stay in Judea. If one subtracts from Matthew the infancy narratives and the
three collections of sayings, seven chapters in all, then the situation is the same
as in Mark. (If John presents a development, then it is, one might say, a
development of faith and unbelief toward Jesus rather than a development of
Jesus himself and of his fate; the point of view figuring in the selection and
exposition of the disputes is certainly not one of historical exactitude.)

The example of two "positive" biographers of Jesus shows how different is the
evaluation of the materials, in comparison with the Gospel reports, when a
"pragmatic" biography is written. Bernard Weiss, at the end of his first
volume, is somewhere in the middle of the second chapter of Mark and the
ninth chapter of Matthew and at the end of the fourth chapter of John. This is
one third of his presentation. The last third of his narrative begins with the
seventh chapter of John. Halfway through his work, Beyschlag comes up to the
sending of the twelve. Weiss devotes less than one and a half of his six books
to the passion story, while Beyschlag devotes only two out of seventeen chapters
to it.

[The "pragmatic" method in historiography was first applied to the writing of

ings in the First Gospel and the constantly recurring controversial discourses in the Fourth Gospel. They all become more detailed (somewhat, considering the time span) only at the beginning of the great passion, with the presentation of his "work." What precedes these sections seems to me to have a different purpose. The purpose is to report not so much *what* happened as *who* acted and *how*. If the author of the Fourth Gospel openly professes to be a preacher (John 20:31), the others are basically no less the same.[12] Even in their narratives they *portray* the Man in his action and intention. What we receive from them is actually only a "character sketch."[13] What else are the narratives—in themselves and for us—but examples of how Jesus customarily acted, what he was like then, and therefore what he is like today? In every drop of the bedewed meadow the light from the sun is reflected; likewise in each little story the full person of our Lord encounters us. The situation here is precisely the same as that with respect to the second article of the baptismal [Apostles'] creed. Some have unjustly accused it of demanding faith in facts, but one should say, rather, that it professes faith in the person whom we know from the facts. If this is true, then all the worries about chronology and pragmatism, about development of consciousness and ascertainable progress, lose their urgency.

church history by J. L. Mosheim (1693-1755); cf. the Preface to his *Commentaries on the Affairs of the Christians before the Time of Constantine the Great* (Latin ed., Helmstedt, 1753; trans. Robert S. Vidal, London, 1813) and paragraph XII of the Introduction to his *Institutes of Ecclesiastical History* (Latin ed., Helmstedt, 1755; trans. James Murdock, New York, 1839); see also Karl Heussi, *Johann Lorenz Mosheim* (Tübingen: J. C. B. Mohr, 1906), pp. 217-18.]

[12] Luke, the "historian," will be cited against this. But so far as his accomplishments are concerned, his critics really rate him no higher than the others; I do not think that his departures from the major course of events earn any special plaudits from them. Besides, it seems to me that in trying to determine Luke's purpose, the importance of verse 4 of the prologue for a proper understanding of verse 1 has been underestimated.

[13] The way Schenkel developed this thought in his book [*Das Charakterbild Jesu*, 1864; 4th ed., 1873] need not obscure the fact that he had a true grasp of this problem. [See the discussion of Schenkel in Albert Schweitzer, *op. cit.*, pp. 205-10.]

In addition we have his words. I shall not attempt to characterize them. They do not need my commendations, these crown jewels of the Christian heart. Many a word he spoke about himself—many more than one would have wished had he been a mere man like ourselves. These words unostentatiously but very sharply distinguish him from us.[14] What he says of himself is in perfect harmony with what he is and does; often his words are needed to teach us how to understand correctly his being and actions. Thus the Gospel portrayal of Jesus becomes for us a confirmation of his self-attestation, and his self-attestation becomes the seal on the portrayal of his nature.[15]

From this perspective we shall also find it possible to concede to the apostolic doctrinal writings that Jesus is capable of doing what they go on to testify about him. They do not exaggerate what we know of him in the Gospels. Nor are they exaggerating when they say things about him which transcend the limits of his earthly ministry, for these things harmonize perfectly well with his inner self as manifested through that ministry. Indeed, these confessions and proclamations of the apostolic preaching give us the clue for appropriating and understanding the Gospel narratives.[16]

It is true that at first glance there seems to be a great disparity between the accounts in the Gospels and the "dogmatic" statements about Christ in the Epistles. Yet they are more closely related than at first appears. The Fourth Gospel is an obvious link

[14] It is well known that Jesus never puts himself simply on the level of other men, not even in John 20:17. Especially noteworthy are the statements in which he imputes to himself the function as Savior from the distress of sin, offers the forgiveness of sins explicitly on divine authority, and takes for granted his claim to the office of judge.

[15] On this point W. Gess's book, *Christi Person und Werk* (1887), is particularly illuminating. How much misunderstanding and futile effort the biographers might have spared themselves, had they, for instance, taken seriously the announcements of the passion and the "idea of the parousia" exactly as they are stated.

[16] F. K. L. Steinmeyer's *Leidensgeschichte* (1868) offers valuable suggestions for this synopsis of what the Gospels and the Epistles say of Christ.

between the Synoptics and the Epistles, for it places its account within the framework and in the light of the most specific statements about the significance of Jesus Christ, statements which elevate him far above a mere likeness to other men. The Synoptics, of course, do not deal with what precedes Jesus' birth; they are all the more specific, however, about the state of exaltation, and it is to their picture of Christ that the infancy narratives belong. In place of the Gospels certain scholars substitute an "original gospel" [*Urevangelium*] without any pre-history, without an "apocalypse,"[17] and without that constant anticipation of the double end [i.e., crucifixion and resurrection] as the real goal of his journey.[18] If, however, we take our Gospels just as they stand, then we find in them the same "dogmatic" character as we find, for example, in the messianic sermons in the book of Acts, those proclamations of the messiahship of the crucified Jesus. For this very reason, until the modern era the church never sensed any disparity between the historical presentation and the dogmatic preaching in the New Testament. If some people have in fact acquired their faith in the Savior from the Gospel accounts without having had their attention drawn to him and their sensitivity to his picture aroused by the apostolic proclamation of the Savior and his work of salvation, be that proclamation in its original New Testament form or in the ministry of the church, then that would only show that exceptions prove the rule. In a time when opinions clash sharply, it may happen that these Synoptic portrayals acquire a special meaning for circles which have become distrustful of "apostolic dogma." Nevertheless, even in these circles one finds a hazy reflection of that dogma, namely, the knowledge of a certain unique evaluation of Jesus within the church, and the attempt to commend his image to our attention and for our approval. The recollection of

<hr>

[17] That is, Matt. 24-25 and the parallel accounts.

[18] Mark 3:6 (Matt. 12:39 f.); Mark 8:31 f.; 9:9, 31; 10:32 f., and parallels; John 1:11, 29, 36; 2:19-22; 3:14-16; 6:53 f. etc.

the days of his flesh and the confession of his eternal significance and of what he offers to us are not separated in the New Testament, even if they are differently distributed between the two types of primitive Christian witness. These two types of proclamation combine to form the presupposition for faith's evaluation of the biblical picture of Christ. We need the apostolic preaching of salvation—of course, not in the sense that we submit to its assurances by sacrificing our judgment and that, as a reward for this achievement, we expect to experience what it declares. Rather, we need the apostolic preaching in order that we might receive direction from our brothers who already know the way by which a person might receive the treasures to be won through and in Christ, first for life itself and then for the understanding. Therefore, we cannot dispense with confessional proclamation if we want a fully authentic picture of Christ.[19]

If we follow the New Testament portrayal of Jesus, we shall see that the Gospels as well as the Epistles frequently refer us

[19] When in the discussions of this subject people speak simply of the Christ of the Gospels, that strikes me as inexact; on the one hand it is too indefinite, on the other hand too arbitrary. Too indefinite, for is John included among these Gospels, and to what extent? Too arbitrary, for if the Fourth Gospel is classified among these Gospels, what prior advantage can it be shown to have in comparison with the Epistles, and with what right? But if only the Synoptics are accepted (quite arbitrarily) as Gospels, how can this selection be historically justified? (In *Beweis des Glaubens*, XXVI [1890], 81, Herrmann says explicitly that he has no reason to regard the Synoptic Gospels as the only source for the portrayal of Jesus which he has in mind; he says "the books of the New Testament." Similarly in *Zeitschrift für Theologie und Kirche*, II [1891], 258, and in the second edition of *Der Verkehr des Christen mit Gott*, e.g., p. 67; if on pp. 90 and 186 he mentions only the Gospels, that is probably merely for the sake of brevity. On p. 185 of the first edition he spoke of "the tradition of the Gospels, as that tradition has been transformed by faith.") It is not only indemonstrable but also improbable, not to say inconceivable, that the Gospel accounts have anywhere had a formative influence on the church without prior preaching of a dogma of Christ, without an assurance of his saving power. Where in church history can we find an example to show that an undogmatic narrative of Jesus has even so much as attracted attention to him? If such an attempt were now to be made, this could not be counted as a proof, since one would be doing it on a field well ploughed by the question, "What do you think of the Christ?" If the term "the Christ of the Gospels" is intended to mean the "historical Jesus" who has to be produced from behind the Gospels, and not the Jesus actually portrayed by them, then the term is more than misleading.

back to the Old Testament and its explicit or prefigurative (typical) prophecy of Christ. And the church in its preaching as well as in its art has interwoven these Old Testament themes inextricably into our picture of Christ. Is there anyone among us for whom the Advent texts and the verses from Isaiah 53 do not form part of his impression of "what the fathers most desired, what the prophets' heart inspired"?[20] These belong to our religious heritage. It is becoming very difficult for children of our generation to recognize and point to these Old Testament roots, while in the historical evaluation and interpretation of the Old Testament a change is taking place which hardly any serious theologian would wholly resist. Nevertheless, the fact remains that Christ can never be evaluated apart from the Old Testament. It is an error to think and say that the situation is one where Christ merely throws light upon the Old Testament. Just as Jesus could appear as the Messiah only among the Jews, so we, too, would be totally unable to appreciate him if we had not been reared on the Old Testament. Among the biographers of Jesus there is plenty of evidence to show that the purely subjective "categorical imperative" does not adequately produce in one a true feeling for the moral example of Christ. Indeed, one may ask whether a Kant or a Carlyle would be thinkable apart from the Old Testament as transfigured by Christ. It seems to me that the sinlessness of our Lord becomes clear only to one whose moral sense has been shaped by the Old Testament world of ideas and men.[21] We must interpret Jesus' references to his Father in a similar way; he would have had to address himself quite differently to pagan people. Also, when we read the words of Jesus, we always bring to them our familiarity with Jehovah acquired from the catechism, from sermons, and from biblical history. I need only mention those forms used in

[20] [A quotation from the German hymn, *Gott sei Dank durch alle Welt;* English translation (by Catherine Winkworth): "Let the Earth Now Praise the Lord."]

[21] Cf. our earlier remarks concerning Jesus' sinlessness, pp. 53 f.

interpreting the saving worth of Christ's person and work which the New Testament and the church have borrowed predominantly from the political and cultic ordinances of the Old Testament. I am well aware of the lively opposition to the use of such forms, which I nevertheless hold to be indispensable.[22] Regardless of how many or how few of these Old Testament references we retain, it still holds true that this Jesus is in fact the Messiah whose Spirit spoke through the prophets (I Pet. 1:11). The historic Christ cannot be portrayed apart from the Old Testament and without taking into account the Old Testament background as well as the Old Testament coloring of his life as he lived it in the presence of, and in, his Father.

Thus every part of our Scriptures contributes its own share in fully portraying Jesus the Christ to us. This observation concerns especially the church's study of the Word. The mature Christian, however, can also come to see the truth of this observation through his reading of the Scriptures and, in private study, can make his own investigation of it by entering step by step into the biblical witness. This is what is meant when we speak of the *biblical* Christ.

In reality, therefore, we are not able to separate Christ and the Bible. We must reassert the validity of the Reformers' protest against all "enthusiasm." The witness of our Bible is woven into every aspect of our developing relation to Christ; in the proper development of that relation faith's view of the Savior is continually clarified and deepened by the witness of the Bible. And in living union with what is already in the Christian's possession the new clarity and depth prove themselves to be such without the Christian's having to subject them to special testing. In this relation to Christ the maturing Christian finds that the distinction

[22] Further discussion of this point may be found in *Jesus und das Alte Testament,* Theses 3 and 4.

between "through" the Bible and "for the sake of" Christ (pp. 74 f.) finally loses its significance.[23]

{The Origin of Faith in Christ}

We want to make absolutely clear that ultimately we believe in Christ, not on account of any authority, but because he himself evokes such faith from us. This thought that *Christ himself is the originator of the biblical picture of the Christ* is implicit in what was said earlier. Let us look at his environment, the medium in which that picture necessarily originated and through which it had to be transmitted. Was his environment receptive to him? Was it capable of knowing and understanding him? The disciples themselves make no secret of the contrary. Indeed, they were even careful to preserve for us his sharp judgment on their own im-

[23] It is a joy for me to add to my discussion here a statement made by a richly blessed "biblically minded" preacher, the late pastor (in Barmen) and my dear friend, Robert Arnold, a man who began his witnessing as a youth. He heard this lecture in person and told me of his agreement with it. After he had received a printed copy of it, he wrote to me as follows:

"To me it is important to observe how the Bible also knows various stages of faith in the Lord Jesus, as you indicated on p. 75 f. [of the first edition]. . . . Something analogous can be said about faith in Scripture. There is a faith in Scripture which is only faith in authority, yet a good and blessed one, possibly based on the fifth (fourth) commandment. It corresponds to the faith of the Samaritans who believed in Jesus because of the woman (John 4). That kind of faith is not adequate during temptation, and so it must become a faith rooted in a personal experience of the living Christ, as in the case of the Samaritans. Then, to be sure, one believes in the Bible for the sake of Christ. However, on the basis of this faith the Samaritans went on to believe what the evangelist further witnessed about Christ (Acts 8). Similarly, a third stage of faith in relation to the Bible grows out of the second, namely, when on account of Scripture and its witness we believe in Christ more profoundly than before, and can say with complete honesty, 'We believe in Christ on account of the Bible!' All this is contained in your lecture, but if perhaps you would state it still more explicitly in your second edition, which no doubt will be issued, the misunderstanding which arises for many biblically minded theologians and laymen who are concerned about the authority of the Bible would decrease." —I know no better way of doing this than by attaching this note to my somewhat more explicit statement above.

maturity in this respect.[24] Their flight and denial ought to confirm their confessions in this regard. As for the others, both Jews and Gentiles—leaders as well as people—immortalized their folly concerning Jesus in the lapidary record of historical facts: they hated and despised him and delivered him up to death. One would also expect that his "image, embroiled in the enmity and affection of opposing factions, would oscillate in history."[25] If now, with due recognition given to their differences, the first eyewitnesses were nevertheless in agreement on the picture of Christ which they handed down, a picture marked by utter simplicity in externals yet far transcending in intrinsic sublimity all that is human, then this picture must have been impressed upon their hearts and minds with an incomparable and indelible preciseness rich in content. They themselves tell us this, and later their lives became powerful proof of how completely Christ had filled their minds and hearts.

This picture has been preserved—as it was conceived—in spite of a carefreeness in transmission almost incomprehensible to our way of thinking. People like to speak of the "assured" words of the Savior; it is a fact, however, that the exact wording of his sayings has gone undisputed only when there is but one account of a saying. This does not deprive the discourses of their authority insofar as their meaning is concerned. Yet they can hardly be said to be marked by an anxious concern to give us an exact transcript of the words of Jesus. The same is true of the main features of his public ministry as presented by the first three evangelists. Al-

[24] The tradition sometimes portrays the disciples as having a definite lack of understanding with regard to his words and deeds (Mark 4:10-13; 7:17 f.; 8:15 f.; 8:32 f.; 9:9, 10, 32; John 2:22; 14:5 f.; 20:9), at other times as failing to understand his meaning fully, so that we cannot say that at this time they had a real grasp of the nature of his work. What is particularly noticeable also is a lack of feeling for his intentions and his power (Mark 4:38 f.; 6:35 f.; 9:28, 29; cf. 9:17-19, 33 f.; 10:13, 26-28 f., 41 f.; 14:4 f.; 14:32 f.; Luke 9:52 f.; John 4:31 f.; 11:7 f.; 13:6 f.; 16:12 f.; Luke 24:25 f.; 24:37 f.; cf. Mark 16:14).

[25] [A quotation from the Prologue of Friedrich Schiller's play *Wallensteins Lager*.]

though their presentation itself, in its one-sided emphasis on the Galilean ministry, remains an enigma, how popular it is nowadays to ignore this obscure point in order not to cast doubt on the reliability of these sources.[26] We cannot dispense with the recollections contained in the Fourth Gospel. Yet we cannot conceal the fact that the author has dealt with his materials very freely in order to make his one great recollection impressive and intelligible for his readers, namely, his impression of the fullness of the Only Begotten of the Father, full of grace and truth, from whom he, as well as others, had received grace upon grace. Nowhere in the Gospels do we detect a rigorous striving for accuracy of observation or for preservation of detail; everywhere we see that the evangelist's purposes have determined how the materials at his disposal are to be employed.

This is the way it was in the circles in which the first eyewitnesses lived and worked. The most effective of all the servants of the Nazarene, though not an eyewitness from the beginning, was nevertheless a witness of the risen Lord. Confidently he emphasizes that he had not received his gospel from men, even while drawing freely on the tradition concerning Jesus' life and teachings.[27] This is more readily understood when we observe how little the witnesses troubled themselves about external matters, and yet how certain they were about the main things, namely, those of "dogmatic significance."

Nevertheless, from these fragmentary traditions, these half-understood recollections, these portrayals colored by the writers' individual personalities, these heartfelt confessions, these sermons proclaiming him as Savior, there gazes upon us a vivid and coherent image of a Man, an image we never fail to recognize. Hence, we may conclude that in his unique and powerful personality and by his incomparable deeds and life (including his resurrection appear-

[26] Cf. p. 49, n. 7.
[27] Gal. 1:12 f. and I Cor. 11:23 f.; 15:1 f.; 7:10 f.; 9:14; etc.

ances) this Man has engraved his image on the mind and memory of his followers with such sharp and deeply etched features that it could be neither obliterated nor distorted. If we are drawn up short by this mystery, then we must recall that he himself solved it in advance when he said: "When the Spirit of truth comes . . . he will glorify me, for he will take what is mine and declare it to you" (John 16:13a, 14).

There is no one among us who knows the course of this tradition in detail. Nowhere does scientific research go back with certainty to the autographs of the first witnesses, who are the sources of our information. And in explaining the relation of the first three Gospels to one another we are still nowhere near a consensus. It remains a complete mystery how the tradition branched out into the respective outlines of the Synoptics and the Fourth Gospel.[28] The more obscure the course of events remains which must have preceded the literary activity, all the more certainly can we sense the invisible hand of Providence over the primitive community's carefreeness in the transmission of the tradition. I am not referring now to the once common assumption of a dictation of the Gospels by the Holy Spirit, which would of course render superfluous not only every form of investigation on our part, but also the whole process of recollection and the connection of the evangelists with the circle of witnesses. Such an assumption would not do enough for us because it would do too much. For such an apparatus, of direct and unmediated communication of the divine truth, would in fact dispense with the revealed God. The

[28] Even if we succeeded beyond all doubt in tracing the origin of the Fourth Gospel to the son of Zebedee, obscurity would still remain. How could the one-sided portrayal that we find in the Gospels of Matthew and Mark come from Matthew the Levite or from Peter and John Mark? In no case was it one of the main concerns of Jesus' witnesses to sketch out a normative model of narrative preaching of his person, a model to be impressed upon the memory of their hearers or incorporated into a manuscript. For this we ought to be grateful. We have examples from our theological literature of what artful attempts to harmonize or criticize, to combine or explain, are able to do to the biblical picture of Jesus, even when carried out with the best of intentions and in reverential love.

revelation, being obscure in Christ himself, would have first been consummated in the writings of his witnesses, who would have eliminated every possible obscurity. In such a view we would, to be sure, come in contact with a miraculous act of God, but we would not encounter the incarnate One himself, his life, his very person. Moreover, it is not really impossible for us to understand Jesus' word of promise. If the communication of the Spirit brings the mind of Christ into our hearts, together with the discernment which that gift brings (I Cor. 2:15, 16), then our minds are opened to what in Jesus' person and work is "of the Spirit." This understanding in turn fortifies the memory and revivifies and brings to full vigor the fading features of recollection, insofar as they express what is really essential. In this way everything is "taken" from the substance of the living, historic Christ (John 16:14).

Thus, whoever concurs with our judgment of the image of Christ that encounters us will also acknowledge it to be a miracle that he was able, within the simple course of an inherently fallible tradition, to make his figure graphically alive, and determinative for the further development of mankind. Is it really a deficiency when the origins of this image remain shrouded in obscurity? No one witnessed the loaves of bread being prepared or saw them multiply, those loaves which through Jesus' blessing satisfied thousands. There they were—real, genuine loaves of bread. Thus it is with all the wonderful works of our God: what we see and have belongs in this world, and we do not know its origin, but what we do perceive we perceive to have come from beyond.

{The Apostolic Proclamation of Christ}

If the biblical picture of Jesus Christ is and does all this for us, why do people search for something more, for another image of him? To substantiate the negation implied in this question, let us try to summarize the results of our rather discursive deliberations.

One cannot make the figure of Jesus the mere object of historical research, as one can other figures belonging to the past. The figure of Jesus has in every age exerted too powerful and too direct an influence on all sorts of people and still makes too strong a claim on everyone to allow a person to suppose that a decisive stand with respect to Jesus is not implicit in a negative attitude to the claim made by the apostolic "recollection" of him, a recollection with which "none of the records of mankind can even remotely be compared."[29] No one can concern himself with this particular slice of history without somehow coming under the influence of its unique significance for the present. Certainly a Christian will always remind himself that the Jesus of history would, or could, be of no concern to him as a Christian if there were not something in this historical reality which concerns him today just as much as it did the contemporaries of Jesus. The way in which the figure of Jesus today confronts men with his claim to be of unique significance for the religion and morality of every person is precisely the way the Gospel accounts portray his encounter with his own contemporaries. It is through these accounts alone that we are able to come into contact with him. They are not the reports of impartial observers who have been alerted to his presence, but, rather, the *testimonies* and *confessions* of believers in Christ.

What is it then that they were able, or deemed wise, to report to us? It was only the activity of Jesus as a grown man. From the sources we know his personality for a period of only about thirty months, at the most, of his public ministry.[30] We know the

[29] Leopold von Ranke, *Die römischen Päpste* (3rd ed.; Berlin: Duncker and Humblot, 1844), I, 5 [trans. E. Foster, *The History of the Popes* (London: H. G. Bohn, 1853)].

[30] Luke, who says he investigated the available sources, was able to learn nothing about the period of Jesus' earlier development. In any case, in the infancy narratives Jesus is the object and not the subject of the events. Furthermore, these narratives have never made it easier for the psychologist to understand the human development of Jesus; instead, they have made it so difficult that in the name of psychology or pedagogy the narratives have either been set aside or substantially recast.

prophet whose initial as well as final preachings make it understandable that his forerunner should have humbled himself so profoundly before him. We know the master teacher who, through what he taught and did, carefully nurtured his wider and narrower circle of acquaintances and brought them, finally, to a decision. We know the resolute Messiah who by interpreting the signs on his life's horizon adhered firmly to his mission and advanced toward the goal he so clearly perceived. We know the royal sufferer whose brief public conflicts show us a man at all times the absolute master of himself, as hardly anyone else has ever been. We know him who rose from the dead, a stranger to his table and travel companions, and yet, at the same time, familiar to them beyond all doubt. We get the impression that what this forceful man said and did, what he imparted to his followers and demonstrated to them, was always subject to his will. We are certainly aware that many things must have happened inside of him of which we hear nothing; isolated clues make us sure of this. It is obvious that those lovingly devoted to him were in a position to preserve many fascinating and winsome details about him, inasmuch as, like ourselves, he lived a busy and active life subject to the routine tasks of the day. However, the recollections preserved by his community give us no information on such matters. Every detail of the apostolic recollection of Jesus can be shown to have been preserved for the sake of its religious significance. Whether or not the religious significance appears to us to be legitimate is irrelevant to this insight. The second evangelist is known for his tendency to "touch up" his account, and yet how brief is even his account, especially when he speaks about Jesus' deeds. How many a person has not read the Gospels for devotions and discovered, at first to his annoyance, how reticent and reserved they are in their reporting of Jesus' words and deeds. Without a doubt the Gospels are the complete opposite of the embellishing, rationalizing, and psychologizing rhetoric of the recent biographies of Jesus. The

"Counsellor" has guided the evangelists "into all the truth," which is Jesus himself (John 16:13; 14:6, 16). Under the Spirit's guidance they remembered Jesus, his words, his deeds, his life. All the chaff of what is purely and simply historical was sifted by the winnowing fan of this pneumatic hypomnesia (John 14:26), and only the ripened grain of the words and works of the Father in and through Christ was garnered into the granary. Just as the Scriptures have forgotten everything that was peripheral to and insignificant for the preaching which establishes faith, so also they draw a veil over Jesus' youth and the period of his preparation for his public ministry. They show us only a sovereign Jesus, master of himself and therefore the quick and unfailing master of every situation, a man who lives life to the full, no longer assimilating from but only contributing to his environment and intent on fulfilling his calling and consummating his destiny.

Let us turn for a moment from the actual contents of his teaching and observe something else instead. His teaching would not mean what it does for us if we did not perceive in it his "authority" (Mark 1:22), if it did not present *his* words and *his* precious spiritual legacy. If we set his prophetic work within the whole context of his ministry, we are actually confronted with only one continuous action: the unfolding and confirmation of his messiahship. Swiftly and concretely he throws into relief the aspects of the messianic question; sharply and surely he draws out the consequences of that question from the motley confusion of opportunities confronting him; and with unswerving devotion he reaches the end of his passion. Pervading everything is the assurance he gives, and the impression he makes, that the decisive thing for mankind, namely, access to the Father, depends upon him, upon his person. He can therefore say: "He who has seen me has seen the Father." Whoever receives a full impression of the personality and character of the Man acting here knows henceforth the character of God (Heb. 1:3). Paul, too, received this impression when he saw him, and it disclosed to him the meaning and value of Jesus' deeds and life (II Cor. 4:4,6; Gal. 1:16; cf. Gal. 1:1; 2:20).

One might say, to borrow an expression, that the Christ of the Gospels is "the transparency of the Logos," with the qualification that this diaphanous medium is not a nebulous legend but a tangible human life, portrayed in a rich and concrete though brief and concise manner. This is, of course, not enough for a complete biography of Jesus of Nazareth; but it is sufficient for preaching and dogmatics, at least for the kind of dogmatics which is willing to leave behind the thorny problems of Christology and instead develop a clear and living soterology,[31] the knowledge of faith concerning the person of the Savior.[32]

The fact remains that the decisive thing in all the biblical portrayals is the twofold ending of Jesus' life,[33] what our forefathers called the "work" of our Lord, though perhaps in a rather too wooden distinction from his person. We ought to learn from the New Testament how to hold his person and his work together. His work is his person in its historic-suprahistoric effect. To know his work in this sense we do not need to be convinced by the methods of historical research. That work is accessible to each of us: in the church as it marches through the centuries, in the confessing word and confessing deed of our fellow Christians, and in the living faith which Christ himself has evoked from us. The passionately held dogma about the Savior vouches for the reliability of the picture transmitted to us by the biblical proclamation of Jesus as the Christ.

---

[31] [In his dogmatics Kähler makes clear that "soteriology" is based on "soterology," i.e., faith's knowledge of Jesus as the Savior. Kähler often preferred the more explicit term "soterology" to "Christology."]

[32] I may be permitted to refer here to my dogmatics, *Die Wissenschaft der christlichen Lehre,* 2nd ed. (1893), pp. 333 f. (*Soteriologie,* part 1). Two of my other writings help clarify the picture of the Savior we have in mind: *Der Menschensohn* (Gütersloh: Bertelsmann, 1893) and *Das Sterben unsers Herrn and Heilandes* (Barmen: Tractatverein, 1894).

[33] [That is, the crucifixion and resurrection.]

What more do we need? Has anyone ever come to a knowledge of Christ by a different path?

We like to summarize our faith and the New Testament revelation in the words: "God is love." How did we learn to make this confession? It was not through the preaching which sounded from the Galilean hillside and was carried by messengers throughout the towns of Israel; it was not from the preaching of the kingdom of God, however much God's love may be contained therein. This obscure metaphor—"God is love"—was first to acquire its full meaning through Christ's deeds and life. "God shows his love for us in that while we were yet sinners Christ died for us," we are reminded by Paul (Rom. 5:8; cf. 8:32-39). And John states very clearly how he attained this knowledge: "In this is love, not that we loved God but that he loved us and sent his Son to be the expiation for our sins. By this we know love, that he laid down his life for us" (I John 4:10; 3:16).[34]

According to the historical content of the Pauline Symbol (I Cor. 15:3-4), it is in the death of Jesus that God has spoken in a language of deeds [Thatensprache] which remains indelible. We need no source-documents to record these facts for they are transported through the millennia by confessions born of gratitude. Indeed, these facts, that is, their essential meaning and abiding worth, cannot be established by historical documents at all; only the witness and the faith of Christians can do that.

Thus, our faith in the Savior is awakened and sustained by the brief and concise apostolic proclamation of the crucified and risen Lord. But we are helped toward a believing communion with our

---

[34] This is exactly what the impressive introduction to the passion story in John 13:1 says when read in the light of John 15:13; 18:8-9 (cf. 10:11,15). This is also the case with regard to other elements of the gospel. Paul measures that obedience which is the root of our salvation (Rom. 5:19) by the statement, "even to the death on the cross." Paul finds the proof that this was an obedience pleasing to God in the exaltation of Christ and in the confession of the same (Phil. 2:5-11). The situation is no different in the Epistle to the Hebrews (Heb. 5:7-10; 2:10, 17 f.; 12:2-3).

Savior by the disciples' recollection of Jesus, a recollection which was imprinted on them in faith, renewed and purified in them by his Spirit, and handed down by them as the greatest treasure of their life. From this communion faith draws its resources to overcome all temptations and finds the means to withstand in all situations and circumstances (Heb. 4:15, 16). In this communion we grow into an inseparable union with Christ (Rom. 6:5; Gal. 3:1; Phil. 3:10, 11), the weakening of which is felt as an attack upon one's very existence. In this communion with Christ we are nurtured—by the picture the Bible paints of him—unto the freedom of the children of God, who still find their treasure to be the abashed, timid, and yet genuine confession: "Lord, you know everything; you know that I love you."

II

Do Christians Value the Bible

Because it Contains Historical Documents?

3

[THE PROBLEM OF HISTORICAL REVELATION]

Perhaps I can best place my view of the Gospels in the right light by candidly reporting how I was led to the position advocated in these pages. In doing so I must indicate the decisive forces in my development as a theologian. However, I do not wish to burden my readers with a mere recitation of my private "experiences." What I shall try to sketch are events which have shaped the whole development of the church and especially of theology during the last seventy years. A person who is a contemporary of these events definitely lacks the capacity to understand and interpret them in a purely objective way. Therefore, the simplest thing for him to do is to set down the understanding he has, thereby acknowledging in advance the necessary reservations regarding the relative nature of his views.[1]

[1] This essay was in preparation when the events in Basel and Bonn caused me to lay aside this work and to publish my smaller books, *Unser Streit um die Bibel* (Leipzig: A. Deichert, 1895) and *Jesus und das Alte Testament* (Leipzig: A. Deichert, 1895). Many of the ideas expressed in those writings recur here in a different context. [In June of 1894 Adolf Kinzler, professor at the mission school in Basel (1879-1908), roused a storm of controversy with the publication of a small piece entitled *Über Recht und Unrecht der Bibelkritik: Zur Verständigung mit ängstlichen Verehrern der Bibel;* in it Kinzler, author of a widely used Bible handbook, outlined his approach to the Bible and argued for the kind of judicious use of biblical criticism that he employed in his own teaching. In October of 1894, during a refresher course for pastors, Johannes Meinhold (1861-1937), professor of Old Testament at Bonn, touched off another controversy with a lecture on the origins of Israelite religion. Kähler responded to these controversies with the two small books he cites in the note. On the "Kinzler Controversy" see Wilhelm Schlatter, *Geschichte der Basler Mission 1815-1915*, I (Basel: Verlag der Basler Missionsbuchhandlung, 1916), 323-27.]

During my second semester in theology, under Professor Richard Rothe's friendly guidance, I began to examine the current literature in order to gain insight into the origins of the New Testament Scriptures. My preoccupation with this task has since claimed a considerable portion of my time, for the exegesis of the New Testament was for nearly twenty years the particular responsibility of my official position. The longer I taught the more convinced I became that, although these inquiries are indispensable, they cannot as a rule achieve certainty in matters of detail. It seems to me that with respect to the New Testament it is impossible to attain that degree of certainty which can, to some extent at least, be achieved in the study of other areas of antiquity. In my opinion, therefore, an honest and knowledgeable theologian will have to admit that the problems of "New Testament introduction" will in all human probability remain largely unsolved. This is not because scholars delight in speculation, but because of the present state of the available means of research. The most convincing efforts to give a comprehensive account of the origin of the New Testament, for example those of Bernhard Weiss and Frédéric Godet, are in decisive points and as an all-round picture no less conjectural than the projections of Ferdinand Christian Baur and Karl H. Weizsäcker. The scope of our real knowledge can still best be learned in reportorial summations of the literature like those found in H. J. Holtzmann.[2] This literary-critical approach inevitably confronts us again and again with the question: Are these writings of uncertain origin able to claim the authority of being a reliable and normative record of revelation?

From the very beginning this question was the focal point of my concern with these studies on the New Testament. Rothe's lectures on the life of Jesus influenced me decisively at the time

[2] [The New Testament Introductions of Weiss, Godet, and Holtzmann were standard works in Kähler's day. Some of the writings of Baur and Weizsäcker dealt with problems of isagogics.]

when I was just beginning to do work on my own.[3] From that time on still another question emerged with increasing urgency: How can Jesus Christ be the authentic object of the faith of all Christians if the questions what and who he really was can be established only by ingenious investigation and if it is solely the scholarship of our time which proves itself equal to this task?

One could deny the validity of this question by objecting that this is always the relation between the essence of Christianity and the progress of scholarship, that dogmatics, after all, stands in the same relation to the Christ of faith as does the study of the life of Jesus,[4] and that it is the function of the trinitarian and christological doctrines to define who and what Jesus Christ actually is. I will not dwell on the fact that this kind of dogmatic study is by and large considered erroneous today, since I do not agree with this judgment. I will grant the validity of juxtaposing Christianity and scholarship and still feel myself entitled to ask my question. With respect to the point at issue here the purpose of all dogmatics is, or ought to be, merely to guard a simple catechetical statement, namely that Jesus Christ is "true God and true Man," against all kinds of attacks and obscurations, past and present. This statement I can hold fast to without the aid of dogmatics. And though dogmatics may grope in uncertainty and may dispute about christological questions, the church still retains the complete and unmutilated picture of Christ painted by the Gospels and the apostolic preaching. Even in the church's darkest hours the creed has preserved the outlines of this picture, and the lectures, translations, poetry, and instruction of the church have kept it somewhat fresh and alive in the minds of Christians. In modern historical research, however, the import of the question "who and what" Jesus

[3] Rothe's lectures on the life of Jesus have not been published. This is unfortunate because they were more worthy of survival than the collection published posthumously as a dogmatics. [Richard Rothe, *Dogmatik: aus dessen handschriftlichen Nachlasse*, ed. Daniel Schenkel (Heidelberg: J. C. B. Mohr, 1870).]

[4] Willibald Beyschlag, *Das Leben Jesu* (3rd ed., Halle: Strien, 1893), I, xxi.

is is entirely different. At best, the divinity of Christ is still a problem for such research, and in most biographies of Jesus the *purus putus homo*[5] is the concealed or openly declared point of departure. The resurrection of Jesus is also a problem for such research. The apostolic interpretation of the meaning of his death and resurrection for us is viewed only as a problem; over against this interpretation it sets the "demonstrably genuine" sayings of Jesus himself. The historical approach is no longer concerned with safeguarding and interpreting a solid core of the content of faith. Only an extremely fluctuating picture of Jesus' personality is approximately certain; approximately, I say, for the outlines and actual features of his life vary continuously with the changing results of biblical research. If questions like that of Jesus' sinlessness, of the clarity of his self-estimate or of his messianic consciousness, of "the idea of the Second Coming," of his lordship over history, or of his seat at the right hand of the Father, must first pass through the filigree of historical evaluation and application of the Gospel materials, then the question arises: How can this figure of Jesus—this tentative residue remaining after the work of critical subtraction—which must now, for the first time, be ingeniously evoked from the mist of the past, be the object of faith for all Christians? And finally, how can this figure have been the object of faith hitherto in spite of this disguise which we are now so "fortunate" as to be able to strip away?

Thus these questions, the question of the normative status of the Bible and the question of the credibility of its portrait of Christ, still retain their validity for me. These two questions, which are inseparably intertwined, basically add up to the problem of historical revelation.

All of us who want to remain—and out of innermost conviction must remain—within the churchly tradition of the Reformers and thus in continuity with the theologians who have held to the di-

[5] [Jesus is "a man pure and simple."]

vinity of Christ are united in our concern for the "biblical" Christ.
For the divinity of Christ, however it may be more precisely defined in theology, means for us: that by virtue of which he may
become the object of faith, without this faith's coming into conflict with the First Commandment and without its leading to deification of the creature. (We are assuming that we may disregard
those spurious uses of the word "faith" which depart from the usage in the Bible and by the church in this respect.) In the phrase
"the biblical Christ" the noun sets the adjective into a class by itself. Insofar as Jesus of Nazareth as the Christ differs from every
mere founder of a historical religion, so too his Bible, that is, the
book of which he is the content, differs from all other religious
books which bequeath to posterity only the sincere confessions—
however exemplary in their own way—of men of vigorous religi-
osity. *The biblical Christ* is the great vital power who has rein-
forced the message of the church from within and preserved it
from the inroads of emotionalistic or rationalistic subjectivism,
namely, from every kind of enthusiasm[6] or mere humanitarianism.[7]
Since he bears the life of Christianity, he also contains within himself the problem of Christianity.

What is then the basic reason a Christian comes to "believe" in
the Bible? What causes him to cling to his Bible with reverence,
trust, gratitude, and a love at least equal to that for his dearest
friend? When he reads this book attentively, he believes that he
stands in the presence of God who there addresses him, just as he
believes that he enters God's presence when he addresses Him in
prayer. The Christian who believes and knows that his prayers are
heard by God is equally certain that he hears God through the Scrip-

---

[6] The word is used in the sense in which the Reformers used it.

[7] Cf. K. B. Hundeshagen, *Schriften und Abhandlungen,* ed. Theodor Christlieb
(Gotha: F. A. Perthes, 1874), I, 159 f. [The reference is to an essay entitled
*Ueber die Natur und die geschichtliche Entwicklung der Humanitätsidee in
ihrem Verhältnis zu Kirche und Staat.* Kähler acknowledges his debt to this
essay in his *Geschichte der Protestantischen Dogmatik im 19. Jahrhundert*
(Munich: Christian Kaiser Verlag, 1962), pp. 139-41.]

tures. If this is an illusion, then—let us make no mistake about it—our prayers are mere monologues. Then we are like the Jews in the presence of Jesus (John 5:37)—we never hear God's voice anywhere. As far as we are concerned, God remains silent; we hear only pious phrases about him. Then it is no longer merely the concern of Protestant theologians whether or not this basic trait[8] in the life of every evangelical, biblically-oriented Christian can continue to be demonstrated to be legitimate and, on the basis of this demonstration, to be reaffirmed and fostered. Doubts concerning whether God speaks to us through the Bible arise from the clear insight—which no thinking person can deny—that in the Bible God uses a variety of means through which to speak to us. Those who ponder this may become disturbed by the "many and various ways God spoke of old to our fathers" (Heb. 1:1) and may take recourse to the "Son." The difficulty, however, is that the Son, too, has only spoken to us "of old," and whether or not what he said has been accurately transmitted to us seems, once again, to be something historical research must determine, since God's accompanying and corroborating witness through "signs and wonders" is not apparent to us anymore (Heb. 2:3-4). In the stress of life one may perhaps always take refuge in the position which had its most notorious expression in Bible lottery.[9] Yet when it comes to giving a responsible answer, there are few people today who, if they are moved to think at all about such a question as this, would look upon every Bible passage as a word of God to themselves without first asking where the passage stands, by whom it was spoken, or in what context it occurs. Of itself the view finally prevails which Luther expressed in the words directed against the false prophets and factious spirits: they come "slavering among the rabble and into the raving and uncomprehending people without any distinction, saying, 'God's Word, God's

---

[8] [Namely, the Christian's belief that God speaks to him in the Bible.]

[9] [The reference is to the pietistic practice of printing Bible verses on tickets which were then drawn from a box and read for guidance.]

Word!' But my dear fellow, the question is whether it was said to you."[10]

{A Critique of Mediating Theology}[11]

With this reminder that the Bible is *not* a catechism, nor a system of doctrine, nor a book of casuistry, nor even a collection of guidances suited to every contingency, it is nevertheless the book within which we seek God's Word. But having said this, we have not solved the problem; we have merely formulated it. The methods which the so-called mediating theology and the revived orthodox theology have used in trying to solve this problem have always seemed to me to be untenable.

The so-called mediating theologians in particular set themselves the task of critically relating the enduring substance of historical Christianity to the impressive developments in the empirical sciences, especially the study of history. Among the theologians of this school are those men whom I and many others of my generation hold dear and to whom we are indebted for having taught us the best there was to learn from our contemporaries. Vis à vis previous studies the mediating theologians tried to state in various ways that in the Bible we come into direct contact with God, for here we are directly in touch with the men to whom and through whom God has spoken. What we encounter first, they said, is Jesus himself. Those of his words which can be shown to be authentic are to be granted absolute authority. Therefore, it is of the utmost significance to us that two of the Gospels have come from eye and earwitnesses, from his apostles. In the second place we encounter the apostles and prophets in their writings. Thus, said the medi-

---

[10] *Erlanger Ausgabe,* 33, 18. [*Ein Unterrichtung, wie sich die Christen in Mose sollen schicken, Weimar Ausgabe* 24, 13; *Luther's Works,* 35, ed. E. Theodore Bachmann (Philadelphia: Muhlenberg Press, 1960), p. 171.]

[11] [Cf. the section on "Die kirchlich-pietistisch bestimmte Vermittlungstheologie" in Kähler's *Geschichte der protestantischen Dogmatik im 19. Jahrhundert, op. cit.,* pp. 118-39.]

ating theologians, almost everything depends on whether or not these writings are genuine, that is, whether they were really written by the apostles. But since the apostles derive their authority from Jesus, on the one hand it must be demonstrated that Paul—who was the most prolific and wrote the things easiest to authenticate—received his "doctrine" directly from the risen Jesus;[12] on the other hand, the "doctrines" of the apostles must lend themselves to comparison with the authenticated words of Jesus. In the third place we meet the authors of the Old Testament and the pupils of the apostles. These must be demonstrated to be in harmony with the first two categories of writings.

Thus the demonstration of a historical connection between the biblical writings and those persons and events credited with the mediation of divine revelation took the place of the unmediated divine origin of these writings through verbal inspiration. These writings were then regarded as revelation to the degree that just such a connection could be demonstrated. This connection was established in part from the tradition and in part from the available documentary evidence. The tradition had to be examined with regard to its reliability. Since the facts had to be established by historical science, under certain circumstances they could just as well be shaken by historical science. Thus one was increasingly at the mercy of documentary research. The results of literary criticism became decisive. The mediating theologians recognized, however, that faith in revelation implied certain inescapable claims, and so thought that in this case one could set certain limits to historical study and require of it certain presuppositions. On the one hand we see in mediating theology a "wait and see" attitude toward literary criticism, and on the other an ecclesiastical and dogmatic restriction of such criticism—the former is fatal to any attempt

[12] Cf. August Tholuck, *Vermischte Schriften*, II (Hamburg: F. Perthes, 1839), 292 f. Cf. also the never ending dispute concerning the word "received" in I Cor. 11:23 and 15:3.

to approach the Scriptures impartially,[13] the latter is inadmissible for a position based upon scientific examination of the sources.[14]

Who among us has not found himself caught in this dilemma? Or can the stopgap offered by our positive apologetics really be considered adequate?[15] Literary criticism raised doubts about the traditional estimate of the Old Testament which the church had uncritically taken over from late Judaism; it also raised doubts about the assumptions of the ancient church fathers regarding the

[13] The danger in this position was deeply impressed upon me through a painful experience. A young man from a pious middle class family, a very thoughtful individual who was unsatisfied with modern rationalism, came into contact with me. During a conversation he had heard Tholuck say that if it could be demonstrated that the Fourth Gospel was not written by John the Zebedean, that would be an almost insuperable blow to Christianity. This statement deeply shook the young man. At that time I was not able to help him with the problem. He descended the ladder of doubt rung by rung, but I hope that during his struggle for certainty he finally broke through to light. The attachment of the certainty of Christian conviction to the unpredictable results of historical research was a stumbling block to this young man, who was looking for a firm foundation. He became suspicious of all "positive" results, i.e., those favorable to the tradition, because he feared that behind them lurked the falsifying influence of faith's demands. Tholuck himself hardly foresaw the consequences of his statement. Since then I have become increasingly certain that my Christian faith cannot have a causal connection with the "authenticity" of the Gospels. While this experience showed me the limits imposed on a mediating theologian by his historical approach, I am hardly ready to regard R. Stier's biblicism as a superior position. Already in his youth Tholuck—"in whose breast Semler later fought with Francke"—saw clearly that neither verbal inspiration nor a double meaning of Scripture [i.e., historical and typical] were able to guarantee for him the indispensable authority of the Bible amid the developments which had taken place. Cf. Leopold Witte, *Das Leben D. Friedrich August Gotttreu Tholuck's,* I (Bielefeld and Leipzig: Velhagen and Klasing, 1884), 236 f.; also Tholuck, *Predigten* (2nd ed.; Hamburg: F. Perthes, 1841), sec. 1, pp. xvii, xxiv f., and his *Rede am Halleschen Reformationsjubelfeste* (1841). [The quotation mentioning Semler and Francke echoes a statement by Tholuck's biographer about his student days at Halle: "The August Hermann Francke in his [Tholuck's] heart gradually overcame the Semler who clamored in his head. . . ." (Leopold Witte, *Das Leben D. Friedrich August Gotttreu Tholuck's, op. cit.,* II, 21.)]

[14] With respect to this commitment to certain presuppositions of faith, mediating theology and orthodoxy are different only in degree. The same is true today, even in the ranks of the so-called Ritschlian school of thought. Cf. Otto Ritschl, "Der historische Christus," *Zeitschrift für Theologie und Kirche,* III (1893), 405.

[15] Even here the upholders of orthodoxy do not differ from the mediating theologians in the main features of their method.

New Testament Scriptures. Then, in reaction, amazing erudition and ingenuity were expended to prove the possibility that those traditional opinions and judgments were after all correct. By accepting the burden of proof, however, the *necessity* of proof was thereby conceded and the legitimacy of negative criticism was in principle acknowledged wherever the counterproof was shown to be untenable. When criticism turned out to be like a never-ending screw, there remained only the consolation that the results of negative criticism would be as short-lived as the traditional views it had debunked—certainly an analogy offering a very fragile foundation. E. W. Hengstenberg, the most indefatigable champion of the traditional view of the Old Testament, is said to have advanced an opinion to this effect. But this kind of reassurance seems to me thoroughly unsatisfactory. Of course, I would not deny that this reasoning has a certain legitimacy for a person who is himself engaged in historical research. I have always reserved for myself the right to criticize that negative criticism which decomposes and deforms the tradition; and because of its tendency to run riot in conjectures it has never gained my confidence. Therefore a theologian who seriously follows these movements in theology may perhaps with reason have the impression that the end results may not necessarily strike a fatal blow to the main assumptions of the traditional view. But how does such an impression benefit the thousands who are unable to participate in historical research? Should we expect them to rely on the authority of learned men when the matter concerns the source from which they are to draw the truth for their lives? Surely Protestantism has been loudly and often enough reproached for being a "church for theologians." Theologians should be the last to claim a privileged position with respect to the holding of independent convictions on just this point of the truth for their lives, nor should they demand that others subject their judgment to the debatable results of theological research as to the magisterium declared infallible by the Vatican Council. And it would be completely wrong if, on this decisive point, our church wanted to imprison its members in the self-deceptions of popularizing scholarship. This warning does not need for its basis an "exaggerated skepticism toward the substantial sum of fully assured results of historical criticism." It is beside the point whether we theologians acknowledge the sum of assured results to be great or small. For whoever cannot critically examine the method by which the results have been achieved can only accept them by an authoritarian kind of faith. To be sure, this is bound to happen in thousands of cases, and it may be harmless also with regard to theological questions. Such faith will not suffice, however, with respect to the basis of biblical authority, as that authority has usually been conceived by us Protestants.

Thus it seems that we have reached an Either/Or. Either we retreat to the standpoint of the seventeenth century—in spite of Kahnis[16] and Dieckhoff[17]—affirming the inerrancy of the external features of the Bible as it was taken over at the Reformation, and rejecting any kind of historical study of the sacred text. Or we deny that there is any essential difference between the biblical writings and other books, and are content to see the biblical writings—because of their antiquity and religious value—differentiated at the most by degrees from other examples of Christian literature. This viewpoint surrenders the canonicity of the Bible and attempts to substitute for it another criterion to determine what is historically and essentially Christian.

At this point someone may protest that this is a doctrinaire point of view. Things are not quite that bad, he may say; the error lies in the rigidity with which the matter has been approached. Let us

---

[16] Cf. Karl F. A. Kahnis, *Die lutherische Dogmatik*, I (1861), esp. pp. 659 f., and his *Zeugnis von den Grundwahrheiten des Protestantisms* (1862).

[17] Cf. A. W. Dieckhoff, *Noch einmal über die Inspiration und Irrtumlosigkeit der heiligen Schrift* (Rostock: Stiller, 1893).

suppose, he may say, that the infallibility of the Bible in secondary matters is surrendered; a reasonable and unbiased person will still retain the impression that a great amount of confidence in the historicity of revelation and in the revelational value of what is historical in the Bible is on the whole thoroughly warranted. But, I would reply, on what does one base such confidence? Certainly one cannot base it on the success or failure of the inquiries and proofs of historical research; for these are always limited and only provisionally valid, that is, their validity endures only until new sources of knowledge appear on the horizon. Then that assured confidence of which this point of view speaks will no longer be the same. The judgments of some are influenced by prejudices which have not been raised to the level of full scientific consciousness. Others derive their confidence from a fuller consideration of the historical setting and of historical movements in general; yet in every such instance other convictions, borrowed or substantiated from other sources and bearing on the essence of religion, morality, and the like, always figure significantly into the results. Despite all the assertions of confidence, literary-historical investigations and other comparative historical studies are so influential today that, with the exception of some very general outlines, everything remains in discussion, in uncertainty, and in flux. No lengthy proof is needed to show that this is also true of the heart and core of historical revelation, namely, of Jesus himself, his person, work, and teaching, and finally also his self-consciousness.[18]

This is precisely what is wholly intolerable for me, and, I have no doubt, for others as well.[19] I cannot find sure footing in probabilities or in a shifting mass of details the reliability of which is constantly changing. Does this really confront me once again with

[18] Cf. W. Beyschlag's preface to his *Leben Jesu, op. cit.*, and his remarks on the most recent literature in this field.

[19] On this statement and on the ensuing discussion cf. M. Reischle, *Der Glaube an Jesus Christus und die geschichtliche Erforschung seines Lebens* (Leipzig: Grunow, 1893), pp. 9 f.

that Either/Or? *Must* I choose between W. Kölling[20] and M. Schulze?[21]

I have never been able to bring myself to make this choice; it has always seemed to me that a decision for one side or the other could never be made with complete sincerity. The great reality of the Bible has always prevented me from simply putting it in the same category as other literary productions. That is to say, I came to the same conclusion with respect to Holy Scripture as with respect to the person of Jesus. By the reality of the Bible I mean what the Bible has been in history[22] and what it has come to mean for my life. Gratitude compels me to mention here the influence which Johann Tobias Beck has exercised upon me in this respect. I should also mention the way in which he taught me to approach the Bible and to hold to it without detailed theories about its nature and origin. What the Bible has meant in history and in my life are two facts which confirm each other. Had I not caught sight of the first and had I not been so powerfully overwhelmed by it, I would not have been spared the temptation to explain away my own experience psychologically and to divest it of its special meaning. Contrariwise, without my own personal relation to the Scriptures, a relation that steadily increased in power and in depth, I would have seen no point in studying that complex history recorded in the Bible, and discovering there these decisive aspects which could become clear and transparent even to a person who must remain a layman in matters of detailed historical research. These facts I was not able to disregard or deny for the

[20] Wilhelm Kölling, *Die Lehre von der Theopneustie* (Breslau: C. Dülfer 1891).

[21] Martin Schulze, *Zur Frage nach der Bedeutung der heiligen Schrift* (Halle: J. Krause, 1894). [Kähler is here referring to the Either/Or mentioned in an earlier paragraph. He cites Kölling (1836-1903) as a representative of the first position ("the standpoint of the seventeenth century") and Schulze (1866-1943) as a representative of the second position ("those who deny that there is any essential difference between the biblical writings and other books").]

[22] This is somewhat more extensively discussed in *Jesus und das Alte Testament,* Theses 1 and 10.

sake of a consistency of logic which accepts as authentic only what conforms to the general norm [*das Gleichartige*] and which thinks it "a sin to tower above the multitude."

{A Critique of Protestant Orthodoxy}

I have found it equally impossible to accept the logic of the claims which Protestant Orthodoxy, in its much debated doctrine of verbal inspiration, advanced with respect to the "attributes of Holy Scripture." Once again it was the reality of the Bible which intervened here, that reality which Hamann[23] so clearly grasped and so masterfully described, a reality marked by the full and unmistakable naturalness typical of human literature and its destiny. As far as we can see—and in the New Testament we can in some instances go back to the very beginnings—the biblical writings originated in a thoroughly human fashion. Why not assume that the same is true of all the biblical writings, even where we lack specific information to that effect? If I believe that the Bible contains God's revelation, would it not be right to learn from the Bible *how* God gives his revelation and sees to its transmission and preservation? Orthodoxy, however, derives its assertions from what it believes *must* be true of the Bible; that is, it proceeds not from the actual data in the Bible, but from those requirements which it thinks it must and therefore can posit in order to have a trustworthy transmission of revelation. As is well known, however, it has been proved by the data in the Bible itself that quite a number of these requirements have in reality become untenable.[24]

Here, too, a rigid consistency has led many astray. It was

[23] Cf. Julius Disselhof, *Wegweiser zu Joh. Georg Hamann* (1871), pp. 118 f.
[24] We cannot go into detail here. I only call attention to the proposition "that the sacred text had to be and has been preserved intact" and place it alongside the controversies over textual criticism and over the vowel pointings in Hebrew. Recently the proponents of Orthodoxy have hailed Blass's discovery of two divergent texts of the book of Acts, because this favors the view that Acts derives from a companion of Paul. But then two inspired texts would have to be recognized, and the fact of their confusion in the tradition would still exist.

thought that only the inerrancy of Scripture concerning every incidental matter mentioned by the biblical writers could guarantee the trustworthiness of the one and only main point. What was forgotten was that this main point constitutes the one great exception which alone will prevent the grace of God from falling prey to human fallibility. The consequence is that wherever such a view of inerrancy has prevailed, whether clearly or vaguely, one's whole faith in the revelation of God is called into question when the accuracy of any detail recorded in the Bible is cast into doubt. And hence the relation of believing Christians to the Bible suffers greatly from an unhealthy frustration.

It is this diseased condition in the life of our church that concerns me. The heart of the present controversy is the question of the correctness of the historical and particularly the literary-historical details in the Bible. Yet, I am not really worried about the historicity of the events of salvation, nor am I too lazy to go into detail in refuting hypercriticism. Nevertheless, I will not take up my pen for this purpose as long as the present controversy—"our controversy concerning the Bible"[25]—continues. Whether the controversy centers on the problem of the date and authorship of the biblical books, or on their divisions or their sources, or on the reliability of the details of the biblical accounts, the arguments and counterarguments always move within the limited circle of our present historical knowledge and method. Therefore they are never conclusive. Anyone conversant in these matters knows also that today we smile at many things which the historical knowledge and method of an earlier day regarded as incontrovertible. Is there anyone who would care to take a stand upon these views from the past? What is offered to those unschooled in historical research can only be regarded as temporary expedients. The exponents of the doctrine of verbal inspiration, not only those from previous generations but the modern ones as well, are perfectly

---

[25] [*Unser Streit um die Bibel*, the title of one of Kähler's books.]

right in looking with disdain upon such efforts. For they are concerned about something that is incontestably valid, and of which we too must take note. Even though we cannot agree with the proponents of verbal inspiration but must seek another way of expressing the unchanging relation of Christianity to the Bible, still the decisive issue is not settled by the controversy that rages to and fro concerning historical details.

The assertion of the absolutely unlimited inerrancy of everything[26] found in our vernacular Bibles has caused a progressive uneasiness ever since the investigation of the traditions of Judaism and Christianity hit its full stride. Who can arrest the course of such investigation, especially if, unlike Erasmus—of whom Luther had a low opinion—one does not "hate the inflammatory truth"? We have the controversy with the Jesuits to thank for Protestant Orthodoxy's theory of the plenary inerrancy of the Bible. When the Roman party, led by Pighius,[27] began to see that they were getting the worst of the conflict so long as it was based only upon the canonical Scriptures, which both sides acknowledged, they became more critical, while Protestants became all the more uncritical of the Bible. When, finally, the Deistic critics began to deny revelation, it was thought that the assertion of a miraculous verbal inspiration would provide a strong bulwark against such attacks.

---

[26] This word has been chosen advisedly. The situation is such that a devoted reader of the Bible has usually felt himself entitled to rely literally upon all the statements made in the headings and subheadings in Luther's translation of the Bible. How reluctantly a person resigns himself to the elimination of the pericope of the adulteress and of the end of Mark's Gospel. How enraged people become when doubt is cast upon the Mosaic authorship of Genesis, etc. This attitude has been partly to blame for the difficulties encountered in connection with the revising of Luther's translation. In England, devotedness to the letter of Scripture produces zeal for a continual improvement of the translation; among us Germans it has produced a certain resentment of any such attempts; and in still others it has inspired the naïve confidence of being able to give Bible readers a more faithful reproduction of the original text, even though the translator may have a most inadequate knowledge of the biblical languages and often not the vaguest notion of the textual problems. These mutually exclusive examples show that the starting point, the same in each instance, cannot be the correct one.

[27] [Albert Pighius (ca. 1490-1542) appealed to tradition alongside Scripture in his controversies with Protestants.]

The result was a bitter attack on the authority of Scripture. The opponent was now no longer another church but instead another conception of God and the world. Henceforth, deprived of a foothold in the mutual recognition of God's revelation in Christ, the whole line of battle began to falter. This shift in the battleline is the beginning of our present predicament. *Vestigia terrent*—the traces we have left behind as we found our way into our present confusion ought not to be hailed as the Ariadne's thread that can lead us out again.

{An Excursus on J. C. K. von Hofmann}[28]

J. C. K. von Hofmann's work *Die heilige Schrift neuen Testaments zusammenhängend untersucht*[29] was grandly conceived. The author employed all the tools of modern scholarship; in no way does his work breathe the spirit of a narrow literalism. It has also contributed greatly to the advancement of New Testament research. Its effect will be still greater when we abandon the superstition that our understanding of the text of the New Testament is adequate and that the only real task remaining is to work with permutations and combinations in New Testament isagogics and theology so as to shed light on the historical setting and thought world of primitive Christianity. Yet von Hofmann's ultimate purpose was to establish the authority of the New Testament by treating it historically. That despite his tremendous application to his task he did not really succeed in reaching his goal is not chiefly due to the lamentable fact that the indefatigable author was not permitted to complete his undertaking. He believed that the canonicity of the New Testament writings could be established by impeccable solutions of those problems which are typical of every age. Had he developed this great insight in detail in a concluding volume, the work in its entirety might have had a greater influence. Of course this approach had already been suggested by von Hofmann elsewhere. What actually prevented von Hofmann's

[28] [This section was prefixed to this essay as a *Nachtrag* to these pages in the text.]

[29] [Vols. I-VIII (Nördlingen: C. H. Beck, 1869-78); Vols. IX-XI, ed. posthumously by W. Volck (Nördlingen: C. H. Beck, 1881-86).]

work from exercising a great influence was the weight which it placed upon the treatment of individual exegetical-critical questions. This meant that the over-all conclusion the work was seeking to establish was derived, unavoidably, from a thousand details, and if the reader finds that only a hundred of them have not been dealt with convincingly, then the majority are of no avail. The induction must be complete or the conclusion is uncertain. The person who is not convinced of the Pauline origin of the Epistle to the Hebrews and of Brundisium as the place of its composition will not be inclined to reconstruct the last part of Paul's life from the proof of the authenticity of the Pastoral Epistles; moreover he cannot let his evaluation of the New Testament depend on a modern proof such as this of the church's traditional view. Nothing in all of von Hofmann's works has been less influential than this reconstructive criticism, which in the competition with the positive criticism of the Tübingen School is excelled perhaps only by the work of Thiersch. Von Hofmann's great work—in other respects an invaluable source— is the apagogic proof of the impossibility of attempting to base the church's evaluation of Holy Scripture upon detailed historical research, because such research remains restricted to the viewpoint of one period of theological development. The controversy between Theodore von Zahn and Adolf von Harnack over the history of the canon furnishes another example of the same. This controversy, ascending to the heights of erudition, makes it apparent that the church's relation to the canon must not be made to depend upon decisions regarding individual points of its history. We must adhere to this principle even when on the whole we may have no doubts about which of the professional historians renders better historical judgments.

{The Way to the Historic Christ}

The subject of discussions such as these is, ostensibly, "inspiration." Their actual content, however, is the question of the inerrancy of the Bible even in matters of secondary importance, an inerrancy guaranteed by verbal inspiration. As soon as one enters into such discussions, one is at first attracted to Lessing's counsel:

if you simply place the Bible alongside of all other books, it will prove itself to be a very reliable and excellent book. Yes, indeed— but it will no longer be the Book of books. It may have been, as Lessing says in *The Education of the Human Race,* a truly excellent primer offering elementary instruction; but then it is not an irreplaceable primer, much less a book without equal even for the most mature minds and for the most modern times.

Why do we take this position? Why do we not share the view of so many of our theological contemporaries who think that the Reformers' stand upon the Bible was only a relic from their past, a fragment they did not manage to discard as they emerged from their shell, that is, from a Christianity of tradition and authority? Using the Bible as a fulcrum, we are told, the Reformers nullified the authority of the church's tradition, and we are following in their footsteps when we abandon even this fulcrum of the Reformers and extricate ourselves from all authority of the past. Furthermore, it is said, for us "historical Christianity" means that Christianity which has evolved from century to century. The Bible may be our most sacred relic, and, to be sure, also the only source of our knowledge of our origins; but the Christianity of Luther is more congenial to us, and our own Christianity most congenial of all. Thus, imperceptibly, Christianity—which is *the* historical religion because it originates from a history absolutely normative, from historical revelation—becomes something which not only has a history but, like everything else that is human, in reality is nothing but history.

In my opinion, although this view is certainly not the vision of a seer looking into the far-distant future, there is something in it which gives us food for thought. It appears as if the one-sidedness that developed—quite understandably—in the fight against the revival of the so-called orthodox doctrine of inspiration has resulted in an uncritical acceptance of Lessing's counsel. There are many who will declare that the inclusion of Christianity within universally human phenomena does *not* correspond to the reality which they know and feel; and it is precisely when they are reading the Bible that they become particularly conscious of the uniqueness of Christianity.

But perhaps that means we are the victims of a false conditioning. After all, one does not *have* to equate the "historic Christ" with the "biblical Christ." It is obvious, of course, that what we know of Jesus comes only from the New Testament; but this does not mean that we have to attribute a special authority to the books of the New Testament. They could simply be regarded as sources. A simple historical examination can derive from these sources a "minimum" of historically reliable facts whose revelatory value is readily discernible.[30] Such a minimum is a "directly attainable datum in the reality of historical life." This has been pointed out to me by various writers.[31] Now, it is not only quite obvious in itself, but there are also examples to prove that a "sound historical examination" comes up with very different views regarding the contours of this "datum in the reality of historical life."[32] If, then, scientifically trained minds arrive at very different summaries of indubitable facts, what happens to the person who is and must remain a layman in historical science? Naturally, the matter presents no difficulty at all to a person who is of the opinion that a true Christian is recognized by the fruits of his neighborly love,

[30] O. Ritschl, *op. cit.,* pp. 409 f.

[31] The quotation itself comes from Ferdinand Kattenbusch (*Theologische Literaturzeitung,* IV (1894), 170). The following discussion is not directed against Kattenbusch, who certainly does not accept only a paltry minimum, inasmuch as he includes the resurrection in this "datum." I mention him only because his picture of Christ, it seems to me, also somehow requires that the Bible have authority for faith if that picture is to be valid for all Christians. For our access to any fact of the past can never be "direct," in the strict sense of the word. Tradition always intervenes. To be sure, a Christianity which is accepted in faith offers what Kattenbusch is asking for. For surely whoever experiences the "Counselor" through the New Testament has "direct" access to the historical datum, i.e., to the Lord, the Spirit (II Cor. 3:17).

[32] Cf. Otto Ritschl's article and Wilhelm Herrmann's treatment in *Der Verkehr des Christen mit Gott* (2nd ed., 1892, pp. 67 f.) with what we have just said about Kattenbusch.

which he may evidence even while remaining unconscious of the fundamental significance of Jesus for his Christianity.[33] An "unconscious Christianity" like the one which Richard Rothe, for example, described and hallowed at the founding of the Protestant Union,[34] obviously has no need of an authoritative tradition about Christ. All a person needs to know is Christ's *Weltanschauung* and its overwhelming power exhibited in the fact that Christianity has continued to exist. To be sure, historical Christianity has usually *not* represented the *Weltanschauung* which people today attribute to Christ—and even today Christianity does so but imperfectly. The Christian with a scholarly bent, however, cooperates in the recovery of an exact picture of the historical Jesus, a picture which, as soon as it was completed, would be the last judgment. Unfortunately, however, the sources are not such that we can hope to attain this goal.—In some such fashion I am set straight.[35]

Certainly, if there is an authentic Christianity—we exclude here preliminary or intermediate stages of Christianity or mere Christianized ethics—if there is an authentic Christianity without any conscious connection with Jesus, and this means without faith in Jesus as the Christ, then one can content oneself with the *viva*

[33] O. Ritschl, *op. cit.*, pp. 385 f.

[34] [An association of German Protestants established in 1863 to win back those increasingly estranged by repristinating movements in the church. Rothe's essay, *Zur Orientierung über die geganwärtige Aufgabe der deutschen evangelischen Kirche* (1862), was a significant factor in its founding.]

[35] O. Ritschl, *op. cit.*, pp. 402, 403. Historical science would therefore attain more with its picture of Christ than Jesus accomplished in his lifetime. Idealistically conceived, it would be the substitute—never to be realized of course—for what biblical Christians in their "superstition" expect from the return of Christ. [In the article cited (p. 402) O. Ritschl argued that such a picture of Christ—while admittedly still far from completion—would be "in a position to demolish all the historical doubts and questions which (a person with) the keenest sensitivity to the truth might raise concerning the tradition." The result would be a "clarification" within Christendom: "all those who are receptive to the divine love in Christ would, without being further hindered by reservations of a theoretical nature, come to joyful and confident faith, while those who still did not achieve such faith would evoke the judgment that they are kept from it by unreceptiveness or obduracy, i.e., by ethical deficiencies." Such a "clarification," Kähler is saying, would achieve what "biblical Christians" maintained would be effected only by the last judgment.]

vox, with the ongoing preaching of the church. In terms of his effect upon our present time Jesus was then merely the founder of a religion or the leader of a school. On the other hand, the person for whom the historic Christ is the object of a conscious inward relationship must be sure that he has this historic Christ vividly before him. Therefore, either he must demand that a reliable minimum or maximum be sifted from the sources and be made available to him, or he must gain a new foundation for his confidence that in these sources he is confronted by the historic Christ, without the midwifery of historical research. So far no one has promised, much less managed, to work out such a minimum or maximum without employing any presuppositions whatsoever.[36] After all, whether or not such a "minimum" could awaken or support faith in Christ is a question which can hardly be determined empirically so long as the Bible and the entire literature of the church, with its wealth of portrayals of Jesus Christ, are not completely devoid of influence. This phantom "minimum" lives from the fullness of the tradition just as the phantom of abstract dogma had done. And like the old dogma it also brings the Christian into a harmful dependence upon theology. This would be even more true of a "maximum," the validity of which could never be tested by the ordinary Christian.

So long as we do not substitute for faith in Christ an assent of our conscience to Jesus' religious ethic,[37] so long as a living Christianity depends on the person of the historic Christ, and so long as the Spirit of Christ identifies himself as such by taking what belongs to the historic Jesus Christ (John 16:14), there will always remain the necessity that we encounter precisely this historic Christ, not as an ideal to be realized in the remote future by

---

[36] According to O. Ritschl, *ibid.,* p. 405, "only a convinced Christian is *a priori* in position to recognize the peculiarity of the Christian religion and of its founder." Beyschlag acknowledges that every biographer of Jesus must make a Christology the presupposition of his research. (*Das Leben Jesu, op. cit.,* p. xxii).

[37] O. Ritschl, *op. cit.,* pp. 385, 414.

scientific investigation nor as the fluctuating result of the biographers' disputations, but, rather, within a tradition which possesses the inherent power to convince us of its divine authenticity. The datum must be "directly accessible." The Protestant Christian's independence of any form of imposed tutelage is not possible apart from the unique place occupied by the Bible.[38] There must be for everyone a reliable means of access to the Christ of the whole Bible, who until now—in spite of all temporary obstructions and precisely in the overcoming of them—has borne the faith of Christians. It is all these considerations, then, that make it impossible for me even to differentiate the "historic" from the "biblical" Christ.

[38] *Unser Streit um die Bibel, op. cit.,* pp. 21 f.

4

THE AUTHORITY OF THE BIBLE

{The Nature of the Biblical Documents}

The "biblical Christ" is still the stone that divides people into two camps.[1] And many whose theological method is challenged by this little book undoubtedly do stand with the author on that side where the watchword remains: the Bible is the unique book it is simply because it "bears Christ."[2]

But then are we not still caught in our dilemma?[3] Not if a way out can be found which recognizes the right as well as the wrong on both sides by showing and correcting the one-sidedness of their respective positions. To indicate this way out and so to remove a cause of uncertainty that has come to attach to the vital point of Christian conviction was the real purpose of my first essay.[4]

It seems to me that we have been too hasty in following Lessing's counsel to read the Bible as we read other books, though naturally our following of it has been from a point of view suggested by the prevailing tendency of our age. Our age wants to see everything "historically." Thus the church's canon of Scripture has become a collection of historical documents. To previous gen-

---

[1] [Cf. Rom. 9:32-33, I Pet. 2:7-8.]
[2] [Kähler is using Luther's well-known expression *Christum treiben.*]
[3] See above p. 108.
[4] [See above p. 45.]

erations the Bible was a revelatory document, a document—as the attempted proofs would have it—of incomparable reliability; to recent generations the biblical canon has become a collection of documents which could be read alongside of others, but, like them, first had to be made accessible through scientific research.

I have never doubted that the biblical writings may and, for certain purposes, must be treated in that manner. If what I have written has been understood to contradict this, then it has been misunderstood.[5] Besides, people hold divergent opinions regarding the possibilities of these texts when viewed from the historical perspective. It is therefore no theological crime if I evaluate them less highly from this perspective than do others. For me the more important question is whether we can do justice to the Bible when we view it from the historical perspective alone. All literary texts can be used as historical documents, even Plato's dialogues or Dante's *Comedy* or Rousseau's novels, insofar as one treats them as sources for a biography of their author or for a history of their period. But does this approach do justice to what these writings have meant and continue to mean to mankind and does it do justice to the original intentions of their authors? I cite these analogies not to define exactly what I have in mind but only to call attention to the problem. I wish to emphasize that this is not a full statement of my views. I definitely grant that in comparison with the examples I have cited the biblical writings have a closer relation to the events they record—and also have more meaning for us—and that it is therefore more appropriate to regard them as historical documents. This is not the whole truth, however. For the biblical writings, or at least most of them, were not written to serve as historical documents any more than were the other writings mentioned above, which I chose at random. Therefore,

[5] Cf. *Unser Streit um die Bibel, op. cit.,* pp. 51 f., "Wogegen streiten wir *nicht?"*

it is one-sided to state that the value of the Bible for the church consists merely in the fact that it is a collection of documents recording the history of the founding of the church. The old doctrine of the inspiration of the Bible is much closer than the one currently popular both to the intention which is dominant in the Bible itself and to what the church has experienced as a result of its possession of this collection. This is also why the old doctrine still has its convinced adherents and why the attempts to bring it up to date in a somewhat revised form do not cease. Nor does this happen only among "narrow-minded people" who know nothing, or want to know nothing, of the last two hundred years of scientific study of the Bible.

I could indeed concede without hesitation that the New Testament (to speak of it first) contains the documents that record the history of the founding of the church. We must understand clearly, however, just what we mean when we say this. The church was founded by the apostolic preaching, and this event is reflected in the New Testament writings. It is common knowledge that we possess no other writings from Christian hands that can compare with these. They contain samples of that preaching, accounts of the work of the well-known or unknown leaders under whom the Christian community established itself in the world, and portions of the exhortations and admonitions of these leaders. The Old Testament also played an important part in this event.[6] Thus we may say that our two-part collection is a document [*Urkunde*] recording the course and the effect of the preaching which founded the church.

But if we go back behind this event to the facts upon which this preaching is based, namely to the "life of Jesus," we find that we do indeed possess historical accounts but certainly not the kind which can be demonstrated to have the value of historical documents in the strict sense of the term. Nor do they themselves

---

[6] *Jesus und das Alte Testament, op. cit.* pp. 22 f.

make such a claim.[7] Thus, we possess no historical documents concerning those specific events in which God's revelation took place—if at all—in the form of historical facts; that is, we possess no historical documents concerning Jesus' public ministry. What we do have is simply recollections, which are always at the same time confessional in nature since in presupposition and intention they always witness to something which lies beyond mere historical factuality—something which we call revelation or salvation. Insofar as those historical facts are treasured by the church, and insofar as the church acknowledges its foundation upon the historical revelation and continually strives for such a foundation, the New Testament Scriptures can, from the point of view outlined above, very well retain a normative authority, even though they cannot be accepted as historical documents for the course of Jesus' life and of primitive Christianity. Then the biblical documents would have a reliability which lies completely beyond proof and which would preclude the necessity of submitting them to a scientific test.

This is the insight which I believe I have gained and with which I think it is possible to put my mind at ease. In order to submit and recommend it to others, I first had to clear the way by rejecting that approach which seems wrong to me. As I said before, however, criticism is not my main intention; my purpose in writing is, rather, to set forth the following exposition, which is not merely negative but also affirmative. For my real concern is, after all, the "biblical Christ"—and not an ideal Christ nor a Christ of dogma. My observations on the Gospels—which may seem overly disparaging—by no means express my full evaluation of them; rather, these observations take the measure of the Gospels

---

[7] Luke's prologue cannot be adduced in refutation of this. A person who does research into sources writes a historical treatise; he does not produce documents, though he perhaps may use them in his writing. The eyewitness of John 19:35 does not collect documents; rather he selects incidents from his memory, with a totally different purpose in view (John 20:31-32).

from the standpoint of a very specific approach to which they have been subjected. While the Gospels are inadequate for writing a "Life of Jesus," from a different point of view they can be regarded as thoroughly reliable and exemplary. This is in fact the way I believe they are to be regarded, as should be evident from Chapter 2 of the first essay.

Perfectio respectu finis (perfection with respect to purpose)— that was the attribute (*affectio*) of the Bible for the sake of which our forefathers believed they could not get along without the hypothesis of verbal inspiration. With this definition, as indeed with perfection generally, everything depends on what is taken to be the "purpose." I deny that the purpose of the Gospels is to serve as documents for a *scientifically reconstructed biography* of Jesus. They have not posited such a purpose for themselves, nor may the church or theology force it upon them as their essential purpose. Their purpose is to awaken faith in Jesus through a clear proclamation of his saving activity. When measured by this purpose I regard them as completely perfect, whereas I deny that when used as biographical sources they are somehow made more perfect through the fact that they are our only available sources for this kind of research.[8] If now we hold that the real perfection of the Gospels lies in their being the Word of God for faith and salvation, and if we further believe the living God to be effectively present in the church through his Spirit, then we will not hesitate to consider the creation and preservation of these Gospels to be the work of God. This work was no doubt accomplished by means

[8] When our fathers taught: *non restat verbum dei non scriptum* (we have no unwritten Word of God), and that therefore revelation coincides with Scripture, such a conclusion was proper and legitimate because they believed it was God's intention to reveal himself and because their admission of this assumption was their supreme presupposition, one they shared with all their opponents. Today, however, people reason as follows: we need a biography of Jesus; we have no sources other than the Gospels; therefore we must regard them as satisfactory sources. Instead, it should have been concluded from the nature of the sources that one cannot produce such a biography, as is true of thousands of cases in history. This is to say: *je n'en vois pas la necessité.*

of purely historical events, which more often than not remain concealed from us, in spite of the ingenious conjectures of scholars.
As a divine event this process is, like everything we call revelation, the object of faith. And thus faith does in fact stand in a
relation to the Bible just as it stands in a relation to the church.
These considerations move me, not only to seek the Word of God
in the Gospels, but also to see in them the Word of God to his
church, addressed to it in a form which it pleased him to choose,
namely through men who in every respect but the one that really
matters here were men like ourselves—of a limited range of vision,
conditioned by the ideas of their time, fallible and forgetful.[9]

Since we are here discussing the "biblical Christ," at first it suf-
ficed to state what the Gospels mean to us. In so doing, however, we saw, in looking at the very heart of Christianity, what our
Scriptures as a whole mean for our faith. The first essay empha-
sized that, with respect even to the heart of Christianity, it is not
only the four Gospels that must be considered. What is finally
said of the Gospels applies in corresponding measure to the rest
of the New Testament books and to all other books of the Bible
to which we are indebted for our knowledge of historical revelation. Even today these books offer to every receptive heart that
knowledge of the living God and of his acts through which it has
pleased him continually to create trust in himself in the hearts of
men.

Earlier we referred to the biblical writings as a document
[*Urkunde*] of the preaching which founded the church; they are
that because they are the record of that preaching as well as the
means by which its purpose is achieved. Of course, this still does
not prove that they must remain for all times the standard model
of this preaching. On the other hand, it can be shown that they
have been not only that but much more, namely, the great source

[9] Cf. August Köhler, *Über Berechtigung der Kritik des Alten Testamentes*
(Erlangen: A. Deichert, 1895), p. 9.

and fountain of renewal for the preaching by which Christianity has grown ever since and, when necessary, has been revived. This *historical fact* can be *understood* in its deeper meaning by the individual Christian on the basis of his own experience. That should constitute sufficient theological justification for assigning a special authority to Holy Scripture. Such a justification will perform a service for the Christian community only when it is content to set forth a fact of the Christian life. It seems to me that this condition is met in the instance before us.[10]

{Three Views of the Bible}[11]

Attempts have been made to exhaust the significance of the Bible in three different respects. It can be regarded and interpreted as a book of doctrinal propositions, as a book of devotion or edification, and as a historical source. There is no doubt that these three forms of the Bible's influence are to be found in history. Do they, however, exhaust the whole historical reality of the Bible?

The significance of the Bible for the Reformers can scarcely be adequately expressed in any of these forms. If its value is to be understood as lying in the doctrinal propositions it is said to contain, as Protestant Orthodoxy maintained, then Herrmann is certainly right in saying[12] that no one consistently uses it that way any more. Reservations are always being made in this respect or in that, as was also tacitly done in the time of Orthodoxy. It cannot be otherwise because the Bible is not a textbook of doctrines and, therefore, when judged in terms of the assertion that it is, it is both much more and much less than that. Luther did not find

---

[10] During the printing Hermann Cremer's three lectures, which agree with the point of view expressed here, appeared under the title *Glaube, Schrift und heilige Geschichte* (Gütersloh: Bertelsmann, 1896).

[11] [Cf. the editor's introduction to the present edition, pp. 30 f.]

[12] *Zeitschrift für Theologie und Kirche*, II (1892), 234 f.

in the Bible a set of doctrinal propositions [*Lehrgesetz*]. Otherwise, rejoicing as he did in freedom from the law [*Gesetz*], he would not have loved the Bible above everything else on earth. Likewise, for him the Bible was certainly not primarily a historical source, in the sense that it first had to be rendered scientifically accessible, since he learned the gospel from the Bible before the rise of the scientific movement and wished only to adhere to the plain word of the gospel. He was certainly not prepared to submit this, the basis of his life, to the unpredictable opinion of any science.

For this reason, too, it is inadequate to call the Bible a book of devotion or edification. "Edification" always implies the building up of something that is already present. No one would call missionary work among the heathen a means of "edifying" them. The Bible is of course an inexhaustible resource for devotional meditation, both in public worship and for the prayers of the individual. But this is not the reason the Protestant churches have made the Bible the really sacred thing in their houses of worship. They have assigned it this place not because it builds up what is established but because it does the establishing. When we look at the significance of the Old Testament for Jesus and his apostles, we see that it is not the so-called edifying value of the Old Testament that is fundamental for them, but, rather, the role it plays in the laying of the cornerstone, that is, in the establishing of faith in the Messiah and our confession of him. In the New Testament Scriptures one may observe the building up of the churches; yet these Scriptures are important for the church only because in the process of edification the basic foundation becomes evident and we see that the laying of the cornerstone also entails the founding of the church as a whole.

In considering the relation of our congregations to the Bible, and basically also the relation of the church as a whole to the Bible, the event in the cloister library of Erfurt, namely, the chance meeting of an individual with the Bible, is not typical—nor was it decisive for Luther either. What *is* typical is that development which, beginning with the suggestion of a fellow monk to hope in the command of God, broke through to an understanding of Paul. It is as kerygma, as a deliverance of the divine commission to his heralds and messengers, that the ancient word of Scripture acquires its significance in the church. This conviction has made countless men willing servants of God. In the missionary work of the church this imperative note of the Word of revelation has been heard, and therefore Bible and missions have been inseparable from the very beginning, with the single exception of the propaganda at the Council of Trent.[13] We do not do justice to the facts of history, and we obscure the relation of the origin of the individual's faith to the Bible, when we view the Bible chiefly in terms of what it has done and can do for each person as an individual. Every attempt to regard the Bible only as a devotional or edifying book, in the usual sense of the term, as a means of deepening an already existing faith, will always provoke the reaction that it will be treated as a book of doctrinal propositions. This is because viewing the Bible only as a devotional book does not exhaust the reality of the Bible. We fail to comprehend this reality if we do not observe the decisive relation of the church's teaching, in all its forms, to the Bible. It is the norm for this teaching, but not in the sense that it is a drill manual or a book of elementary pedagogy. The Bible is, rather, the authority which sets forth the duty, the right, and the contents of independent teaching in the church. It is the norm in the way that the germ in a seed is the "norm" for the blade and the ear; that is, in its germinating stage the seed bears within itself the formative power of its later develop-

[13] [Kähler here seems to be alluding to his distinction between mission, as the proclamation of the gospel, and propaganda, as the propagation of a specific form of Christianity. See his *Dogmatische Zeitfragen*, II (1908), 347; also Wilhelm Oehler, *Geschichte der Deutschen Evangelischen Mission*, II (Baden-Baden: Wilhelm Fehrholz, 1951), 42.]

ment. The ideal of beauty is experienced as a law by one unequal to the ideal. Or more correctly, the art of a Raphael is sensed as a law (that is, as a crutch or a chain) by one who is not able to penetrate its living beauty. The person of Christ is law to me until he sets me free. The Bible is "the letter" to one who does not stand in a living connection with the work of the Spirit (II Cor. 3). Certainly the teaching of the church does not come into being apart from doctrine, apart from statements concerning what there is to know; but in no sense can it be reduced to a tradition of doctrinal information. Indeed, this is not even the chief function of the church's teaching. It is equally certain that the significance of the Bible for the teaching of the church cannot be encompassed by the formula "doctrinal propositions." Nor can we define the relation of the Bible to teaching by calling the Bible the "classic model" of teaching, since such a definition does not adequately express the productive role played by Scripture.

It is my opinion that in the church's teaching we are still too much inclined to give one-sided attention to what has been fixed in dogmatic definitions. One must not overlook the fact of the reading of the Bible, as soon as it is available in the vernacular. Our great poets did not have to wait to become influential until the critics began expounding them, discovering many words which were hard to understand and which, to be sure, had till then hardly ever been clearly understood or interpreted with any assurance. Likewise the effect of the reading of the Bible has not been bound to correct exegesis and a perfect capacity of the hearers and readers to understand the meaning of the text in its historical setting. Preaching from the Bible, moreover, has kept alive many things in the Bible which did not find their way into our textbooks. A very faithful adherence to the Bible has borne fruit even under gravely obscuring circumstances. Here the history of preaching and of the literature of asceticism is instructive.

These are suggestions which seek to indicate how the canonical relation of the Bible to the teaching of the church is based upon a certain setting in reality; that setting is not fully acknowledged when the Bible is called merely the oldest record of the facts which are significant for faith and, therefore, also for the preaching which promotes faith. The actual situation is rather that all Christian proclamation has developed directly or indirectly from the way in which the Bible conceives the significance of these facts and witnesses to them with a view to evoking faith and the evidence of faith in life. Such Christian proclamation has been profitable to the extent that it directly, and with real understanding, followed this lead of the Bible. That this is the actual situation is so easily concealed from many of our contemporaries only because our cultural world, especially since the Reformation, is saturated with the themes and implications—one could find more apposite expressions—of the biblical word. Naturally, this is especially true within the ecclesiastical and religious spheres, but it is plainly true not only of them but of our spiritual and intellectual life as a whole. Here we should also not forget that all the attacks on biblical Christianity—as deplorable and detrimental as they may be—are themselves dependent on the Bible, a book the attackers know with their minds if not with their hearts. Much worse is the polite disrespect which acts as if the Bible were no longer worth discussing or no longer a topic of discussion.

This dependence upon the biblical word is inherent in every form of the church's teaching. This is as true of the theology enunciated by that teaching as it is of its actual practice in awakening, preserving, and cultivating faith. Apart from the church theology and practice fall into fatal arbitrariness; apart from the Bible they condemn themselves and those they serve to spiritual atrophy. That is because the church's teaching is not the product of religious consciousness. All the founders of religions may have had original thoughts about God. But it is the authentic Word of God that the believing Christian encounters in the Bible, a Word spoken on God's authority and deriving its substance from him. Whatever the Christian may have encountered previously or elsewhere remains a derived Word of God, no matter how powerful the conviction with which it was received and propagated, no matter how certain was the impression of both speaker and hearer that it was spoken on God's authority.

To be encountered by this Word, and to grant to it authority over one's own mind and will, is certainly a matter for each individual to experience for himself. The correct sequence is never this: first to acknowledge the form and then the substance, that is, first to declare that this book is revelation and then to appropriate its contents for oneself. This is just the trouble with a set of doctrinal propositions [Lehrgesetz] insofar as it is imposed on faith as a law [Glaubengesetz]. Such an imposition requires a fides implicita—not, to be sure, with respect to the church, but required by the church. Then the question necessarily arises how far this legally constituted Word of God extends. The familiar discussion about "the Word of God in the Bible" has raised just that question: Is everything in the Bible the Word of God[14] or only some parts of it which have yet to be determined? Given the second alternative, it follows quite consistently that the determination should be made legally, and therefore mechanically; for example, by limiting God's Word to those passages where it is explicitly stated, "God said" or "Jesus said." Then immediately the uncertainty arises as to where, exactly, such statements are to be found in the Bible.[15] Nevertheless, even though this procedure is incorrect, it surely cannot be denied that in using it—perhaps in spite of it, yet without a doubt while using it—many people have come to a living faith in the Savior. This is possible because here we are merely confronting a wrong formulation of an incontestable fact, namely,

---

[14] This differs from the assertion that the *whole* Bible is God's Word, which excludes the divisibility of God's Word into parts. The other statement asserts the equivalence of all parts.

[15] That the same is true of Jesus' words requires no lengthy proof.

that no one, apart from a few isolated exceptions, has surrendered himself in trust to the Word of God, unless others—if only the biblical writers themselves—have first proclaimed to him that here is the Word of God and that it is now up to him whether he will also believe it. Such a proclamation does not necessarily lead to a sacrifice of the intellect, brought on by the desire to purchase peace and assurance. It is intended, rather, as an invitation and as a pointing out of the way. The details of how faith becomes lasting I shall not discuss here. In any case the result must accord with I Corinthians 2:5: "That your faith might rest upon the power of God." We do not believe because of the church, but through the church and in the church. If it is true that we would not have come to the written Word nor to steep ourselves in it had it not been for the "living voice" of faith (the Word of God constituting the content of that faith), then we cannot flatter ourselves for having a private and privileged relation to it. Nor do I as an individual have any right to declare that the particular way in which I personally came to faith in this Word is the only possible one, or to state that what has become decisive for me is the only important or even the most important thing. Here we should add that the written Word does not exist merely and primarily for isolated individuals but for the living totality of the church and its members.

This totality, the church of Christ, cannot, however, adopt for itself the standpoint of those who are just becoming Christians; it cannot tailor its teaching to fit the situation of those who are only seeking to become Christians or to acquire faith, and who as individuals have yet to discover the authority of the Bible for themselves. Therefore the church acts and witnesses as the totality of believers for whose faith the written Word has obtained authority as the Word of God. Furthermore, the church cannot overlook the fact that it hearkens back not only to a series of isolated experiences of faith by its present members but also to a long his-

tory of God's leading of the church. Nor can it overlook the fact
that for the understanding of this history illumination is not lacking in the written Word, and that this is a history which the
present members of the church find is substantiated by those experiences which repeat themselves in every age in relation to the
Scriptures.

In the life of Christianity, both as it occurs in individuals and
in the great church movements, we cannot but observe the fact
that we possess in the Bible the instruction intended and given by
God concerning his coming to us and our coming to him. It is an
instruction which comes to us with all the dynamic power that accompanies a gift and action of the living God. It does not remotely
resemble a set of doctrinal propositions; rather it places us in a
rich world which grows and develops in length and breadth under
the revelation of God. As we concern ourselves with this sharply
etched history, we find that the great deeds of God and the person of his Christ become contemporary for each one of us, making
of us first hearers, then learners, and finally believers. The Bible
presents this history again and again to those who teach in the
church, admonishing them on the highest authority to place themselves in its service. These observations confirm the result of our
earlier inquiry which showed in what respect our biblical writings
are historically valid, namely, as a document of the preaching
which founded the church. And this confirmation bolsters our assumption that we have thus gained the true foundation for the
authority of the Bible. This is not a foundation which rests upon
detailed scientific research or upon an individual Christian's rati-
ocinations on the biblical books or materials, with the majority of
Christians being left in the position either of simply concurring
or of groping aimlessly in the dark. But if confidence in the divine authority of Scripture has once been regained, then the
measure and manner of application can be derived from the relation for which and the way in which this authority is established.

The way in which the creative authority of the Bible (*auctoritas efficiens fidem*) is approached has always determined the foundation of the judicial authority of the Bible (*auctoritas iudicativa*). Wherever and whenever that creative authority has been operative, Scripture has also been handled correctly—not according to rules, whether ecclesiastical or scientific, which can be mechanically applied, but from an understanding which grows out of a life that is constantly being renewed.

These three views of the Bible—as a book of doctrinal propositions, as a historical source, and as a book of devotion or edification—are offered to languishing, brooding, and quarreling people, among whom a remnant of believers toil and struggle for existence, and to others who are trying to find their way back to their spiritual home. Because of their one-sidedness, these views actually turn out to be false. As soon as we look beyond them, however, to our restless and stirring times, which, rather than seeking a formula, live and act out of experience, then we discover that none of these views does full justice to the facts; each in some way obscures them. What we also see clearly, however, is the creative authority enjoyed by this uniquely real and, in every respect, marvellous tradition in which God reveals himself, speaking to us in history and, finally, in his Son.

{Two Tasks}

Naturally we should not conceal from ourselves that one can speak of a special authority of the Bible for Christians only if one actually accepts revelation and, in addition, assumes that there exists between this revelation and the biblical writings an extremely intimate relationship, the exact definition and description of which we may for the present postpone. Surely this is what the older mediating theologians had in mind, as did their disciples when they referred to the biblical writings as "documents of revelation." The basis for biblical authority, they maintained, was not the demonstrable antiquity of the Bible but its origin from mediators of revelation.[16] It only confused matters when it was thought that this connection between the Bible and these mediators had to be demonstrated by a synthetic construct based on exhaustive investigation of details. Here the uncertainty lodged. If it is possible to unravel this entanglement of authority with historical demonstration, then both tasks[17] can be carried out peacefully side by side. There is absolutely no point in wanting to prove the authority of the Bible to people who neither can nor want to consent to a revelation. With them we have another task, of which more will be said shortly. But with the person who is not bent upon denying revelation, we may further discuss the scope and nature of revelation as well as the manner of its preservation. His eyes and his mind can be opened to the great reality of the Bible and of its efficacy, a reality in which—as in the biblical revelation itself—a Spirit, transcending the merely historical, can be perceived as operative in tangible historical events.[18] I call this the testimony which the Spirit gives *in the church* concerning the written word of God. This testimony is frequently instrumental in engendering the testimony of the Spirit in the hearts of individual believers (the testimony which is usually exclusively stressed); in any case, it confirms, supplements, and supports that testimony.[19] This "demonstration of the Spirit and power"[20] takes place by no means solely with reference to the living voice of the gospel, but at least equally as much with reference to its written form. Our

[16] [See above pp. 106-7.]

[17] [The task of giving new insight concerning the Bible to those who accept its authority and the task of opening its pages to those who do not.]

[18] *Jesus und das Alte Testament, op. cit.,* Thesis 12.

[19] See *Die Wissenschaft der christlichen Lehre,* 2nd rev. ed., par. 51.

[20] [I Cor. 2:4. The phrase used here, *Beweis des Geistes und der Kraft,* is no doubt an allusion to Lessing's famous piece *Über den Beweis des Geistes und der Kraft,* in which the oft-quoted sentence appears: "Accidental truths of history can never become proofs of necessary truths of reason."]

fathers did not go astray in assuming this; they erred only in restricting this demonstration exclusively or at least particularly to the written word. Moreover, there is among us no such "living voice" which does not derive, directly or indirectly, from the Bible. Thus the normative authority of the Book in which it pleased God that the primitive preaching should be delineated can be quite adequately established for believing Christians, in the manner we have tried to indicate, without having to elucidate obscure facts of the past. Only faith's evaluation is necessary, a historical fact which is beyond all controversy and which, moreover, has repeatedly recurred throughout the entire Christian era until this very day. That is the situation; for the fact that we know of no form of Christian preaching older than our Bible is, from the standpoint of *historical science,* more certain than the fact that Jesus of Nazareth ever lived. Whatever other literature one may—if one adopts the most extreme critical views—regard as contemporaneous with the New Testament, none of it has either then or in the long run served to establish and build up the church. And what called forth and constituted the Reformation and every new awakening in our churches has always been the revival of faith in, and of preaching from, the written word of God.

This view of the Bible goes far beyond that mentioned earlier which says that the Bible is merely the "classical literature" of our religion. One might perhaps raise questions about this "classical" view at one point or another; yet it would still be usable in a limited way. But the view we have been developing strikes much deeper into the life of the church and of its members. The value of our Bible is for us grounded in that in which our Christianity itself is grounded. The value our Bible has for us was and remains inextricably interwoven with the creative means of grace, with the Word of God as it has arisen in history and done its work there. This Word is superior to other gifts and dispensations of God in the same way that his self-revelation to us is superior to the hand of his providence. It should also be apparent that the above interpretation has the great advantage of being in agreement with the Bible's own evaluation of itself. For in the Bible the Word of God is the transmission of revelation, even for those who themselves receive revelation and speak the Word of God. What these recipients understand by that, however, is precisely the living Word, the life-giving and life-determining self-disclosure of the living God which comes through human speech in all its conceivable forms.

A person who holds this view stands just as solidly upon the authority of the Bible as does any advocate of verbal inspiration—except that he does not have to take upon himself the burden of proving the details of the tradition regarding the biblical books, a burden always acknowledged by the advocates of verbal inspiration. Without apprehension or anxiety he can grant to historical research all the freedom it desires, to investigate the compilation of the biblical canon and the age and literary construction of the books and portions thereof. He will be confident that Achilles' lance will possess healing as well as wounding power. It is our opinion that historical research will itself refute its own excesses, where there have been such, and will demonstrate their erroneousness.[21] The incentive to such excesses will be largely dead when the radical opposition between the acceptance and the denial of revelation no longer plays a decisive role in these discussions, or as soon as a proof of the inauthenticity or historical inferiority of a portion of the Bible is no longer considered an

[21] To this extent I fully accept A. Köhler's concluding words (*op. cit.*, p. 68): "not rejection of criticism, but criticism against criticism." However, I think that this kind of reflective criticism cannot satisfy all the justified claims of the opposition. It is this extra something that I am trying to offer, here and elsewhere. Obviously I do not think that a person should merely leave criticism and its practitioners to themselves and wait until it corrects itself. Otherwise I would not have published this book either in the first or the second edition.

essential link in the proof against the truth and "supernaturalness" of Christianity itself.

There are, on the one hand, some who suffer the disavowal of this supernaturalness because they are unable and unwilling to deny what is evident to them. Such a denial of revelation is not the goal for which they strive, however. Why is it then that scholars repeatedly point out the errors in the traditional text of the Bible? Why do they put their fingers on the contradictions revealed by the narratives or by the conceptions contained in the ancient sources that have been made a part of a certain book? Why do they spend time proving that historical statements in the books do not correspond with the conditions of the time to which the tradition ascribes their origin? They do so chiefly, do they not, to secure the right and freedom of literary criticism. If it were no longer necessary to establish this right and freedom, then leisure and freedom from bias would increase and would make it possible to observe how, despite all historical relativity of form, the uniqueness of the biblical content nevertheless guarantees the reality of what is peculiar to it, namely, the revelation it presents. It would also be observed what amazing agreement is evident in all the stages, and amid the diversity, of this religious development; yes, how in fact even from the standpoint of criticism the biblical writings stand out conspicuously—as Lessing was right in emphasizing—from other comparable legacies from antiquity, not miraculously different in kind but different in degree. Scholars would find that composure which opens one's mind to the other side of a question. No longer fearful of revived efforts forcibly to harmonize the biblical accounts, they would evalute the age of the Hebraic writings more impartially, as has already happened in the field of New Testament research, and they would discover, to their delight, the agreement of the biblical records with other historical evidence. Once the infallibility of our biblical records is no longer demanded, then their comparatively remarkable trustworthiness will again be appreciated, even the truthworthiness of the legends,[22] so far as this is conceivable.

On the other hand there are "Bible lovers"[23] like Menken who suffer all the anguish of the defense—a defense which frequently does not even relate to the actual text but only to some traditional misunderstanding or lack of understanding of the same—because they are afraid that otherwise they will be deprived of trust in special revelation. If they could once be relieved of their anxiety that the written Word of God as such can be devalued for them, and if it once became clear to them that their biblical Christianity would remain secure even if our historical knowledge *about* the Bible and its origins were in fact much less certain than they had previously thought, then they would very soon learn to be content with this minimal historical knowledge because of their rich measure of a real knowledge of truth. They would learn to make, consciously and confidently, a distinction in their Bible. There always were for them many things in the Bible not essential to their spiritual life. However, they accustomed themselves to wringing something even from these sections, in the belief that this appertained to the correct use of the Word of God as a whole. A certain delight in the play of ingenuity, which passed itself off

[22] Offense has been taken at my use of this term [*Sage*] in *Jesus und das Alte Testament*, pp. 51 f. I was told that I should rather have spoken of "oral tradition," or, still better, of "witness." But it seems to me that, precisely for the sake of our discussions about the historicity of the biblical facts, it is important for us to see that there is no sharp conceptual difference between oral tradition and legend. The difference is not even fully secure and beyond debate when we consider the generation which followed the ear and eyewitnesses. Hebrews 2:3 does not say merely "transmitted" (Luther: *auf uns gekommen*) but "confirmed" [thus now the *New English Bible*], i.e., transmitted in a reliable legend. Thus the reliability of the earwitnesses is in this case something special, needing the testimony of God.

[23] [*Bibelverehrer*, a term Kähler took from Gottfried Menken (1768-1831), a Reformed pastor in Bremen. The basic characteristic of the *Verehrer*, said Kähler, is that in the Bible they hear "God speaking to (them), and not merely other pious people speaking about God" (*Unser Streit*, p. 2). Kähler addressed his booklet *Unser Streit* to the *Bibelverehrer*, "since I believe I am able to put myself in their shoes and to sympathize with them in the present unrest" with respect to the Bible (*ibid.*).]

as profundity, no doubt supervened. If their view of the Bible as the Word of God to man no longer required that every fragment of its contents must prove to be equally and readily applicable to every person, then there would also vanish this artificial enthusiasm for what proves to be "dormant" material for the reader in his actual living relation to the Bible. Then the meaning of Luther's words would also be disclosed: "the Bible is the book given by God the Holy Spirit to his church."[24] Then it might become evident that the Bible is not the classic example of devotional literature, but rather the normative source of the teaching of the church. Whoever grasps this insight and pursues it further will also understand the intrinsic significance of that "dormant" material and why it is in our Bible, even though not every single passage can, without torturous and artificial efforts, be made edifying for the individual.

How can we make the Bible accessible to those who deny all revelation? In looking about for a promising approach, we must keep one thing in mind from the start. Where a conscious denial of revelation exists, it is always the result of a spiritual and intellectual development which has carefully considered the questions of the possibility and the reality of revelation. Not every vociferous denier has done this; yet such a person walks in the footsteps of predecessors who have seriously concerned themselves with these questions. Within our own situation all such tendencies have in one way or another already settled accounts with Christianity. All attempts to confront such opponents by first imposing upon them the miraculous character of the Bible, and then proceeding to derive from it the revelatory value of its contents, have long ago proved unsuccessful. A normative authority of Holy Scripture

[24] Cf. *Unser Streit um die Bibel*, p. 12. [The Luther quotation is from *Exempel, ein rechten christlichen Bischof zu weihen* (1542), *Weimar Ausgabe*, 53, 252.]

cannot be the presupposition for acknowledging revelation, but solely an implication of it.

Nevertheless, the Bible itself can awaken faith in revelation even when it is read divested of all authority, for it places before us the fact of revelation just as clearly—and just as unclearly—as Jesus, the prophets, and his apostles once did: "Whoever is of the truth hears my voice" (John 18:37, 3:19 f.). Our task will be simply to remove or weaken the obstacles which the faults of the visible church—but also, and equally, the grave errors of an unchurchly and anti-churchly culture—place in the way of unprejudiced reception of the impression which the Bible can evoke. The means to this end will be quite varied, especially if the previous history of each individual is taken into account. Yet one rather fundamental difference may be recognized. By far the great majority of opponents appeal to scientific scholarship and to the negative verdicts it has pronounced on the view that the Bible has any special worth or, *a fortiori,* contains a revelation. There is nevertheless a great difference to be found among these opponents; one can approach those trained in scientific studies differently than one can those who are merely blind adherents of such study, and in a certain sense the task is easier with respect to the former.

We shall always have to keep in mind that our only valid task is to bring these persons into an unprejudiced contact with the Bible. We shall therefore require no concession from them in advance but start instead with the indubitable fact which we have already stressed (pp. 124 ff.). We must go to the content of the earliest preaching and, starting with a "minimum" of what can be historically ascertained, introduce them to problems which serious research cannot easily dismiss. If they decide to demolish the problems on intrinsic grounds, then at least the decision is removed from the sphere of empirical science and its alleged "inviolable truth." Then another kind of conflict begins. But frequently it will be possible to open someone's mind to the fact that in just these problems cues can be found which compel serious reflection on the fullness of the biblical contents.

Even so-called educated people are less acquainted with historical research itself, however, than with some of its results. Our contemporaries, who are "accustomed to viewing things from a historical perspective," rarely have a real understanding of the conditions of historical knowledge. From the higher ranks of society to the mass of lower classes people have an idolatrous regard for infallible science and give their blind assent to its most recent or, depending on one's range of vision, even to its obsolete achievements. These circumstances force us to fight hard against this all-powerful prejudice; it is a fight that must be fought. To remove some widespread prejudices by superior argumentation is useful. But documentary research cannot successfully be demonstrated to those who have not engaged in it. To impress them with authorities, to hold up before them distinguished scholars who judge the Bible differently from themselves, all this can only lead to a vague deference to authority, which is soon disposed of when more congenial authorities are introduced. Anyway, people are not of late attracted to belief based on authority. Indeed, only a preliminary and pedagogical importance is attributed to it. In our defense of the Bible and our correcting of false opinions in the face of the often very cleverly concocted calumnies of the Bible, we shall be more effective and on surer ground if we carry on these tasks in a way that brings the real nature of the Bible into view and displays the richness and the incomparable uniqueness of its contents before people so that their minds, although alienated from the spirit and tenor of the Bible, may again be opened to it and they may once again see everything with their own eyes. All work of this kind must be done with the definite aim of making oneself superfluous. There is so much—indeed, too much—arguing back and forth about the Bible and Christianity. The particular way that is used to put an end to this squabbling does not matter too much. If in our day, which is so saturated with reading material, we could once succeed in inducing a considerable number of people to feel inclined to *read* the Bible, then we would also have the occasion to teach them *how* to read the Bible again.

To bring the masses under the educational influence of Christian and churchly presuppositions, so that they might then find their way to the heart of evangelical faith, is surely a goal which today cannot be achieved and therefore should not be striven for. This is also true of any presupposition in favor of the Bible. It must be considered enough that each person is confronted by the Bible in its inseparable connection with Christianity and the church. If the Bible itself can be made accessible in the way we have indicated, then a person's ultimate decision will never proceed from intellectual deliberations but always from a serious quest for a message from above.

The fact of biblical criticism—a phenomenon now two and one half centuries old—does more than merely present us with problems and tasks. An acquaintance with biblical criticism also makes us, it seems to me, more skillful in resolving these problems than we would be if we approached them from the standpoint of our orthodoxist forefathers. Even those laymen who are well versed in the Bible, and so do not have to lean on others in their reading of it, stand under the direct influence of biblical criticism more than they themselves realize. If previously the Bible appeared as a broad homogeneous mass offering in every passage an infallible oracle, today, in continuing response to new developments in criticism, people have become aware of the structure of the Bible's contents. The great facts of the Bible and its vivid personalities have emerged as significant, not only inasmuch as they satisfy our simple desire for the graphic and concrete, but also for our questions and reflections on matters of divine and human import. Interest in historical links, details, and means of presentation has receded into the background and comes into the foreground again only when the controversy over the infallibility of the Bible flares up again and again. Today the attempt is made first of all to place oneself in the past so that, having gained a fuller understanding of the original meaning of words and events, one may recur to one's own thinking and to the application of the original meaning to one's own life. The Life-of-Jesus movement, one very definite aspect of which we attacked in our first essay, is on the one hand the result and symptom of this procedure; on the other hand it has helped to make the person of our Savior, in the vivid manner in which the Bible portrays him, the focal point of all biblical research and all reverent use of the Bible. The very person who recognizes the significance of this movement for the church's task under discussion in these final pages will—as is here attempted—be all the more concerned that at this focal point of our battle array serious blunders should be avoided. But if it is true that there is now an awareness of the historical gradation and the historical diversity of divine revelation and the responses to revelation, and if as a result there is also a willingness to make the abiding contents of revelation stand out from the changing forms of expression, then a freedom of movement has been created which enables us to meet the deniers of revelation halfway in order to introduce them wherever possible to the focal point of revelation, and thence to the fullness of historical revelation as well. But this freedom of movement would of course offer little hope of success if it did not proceed from a firm starting point, namely, from a sense of confidence in the normative, unchangeable content of the church's teaching, namely, in the Bible as a whole; this is a starting point at once historically unassailable, grounded in faith, and independent of scientific scholarship, however much it is the task of scholarship to circumscribe this starting point.[25]

It is out of these experiences, impressions, observations, and reflections that the first essay in this volume originated. It lays hold of the problem of historical Christianity at its focal point, and nothing is more remote from it than "the dismissal of the truly vital question of all theology by the self-confidence of a practitioner of the latest dogmatism."[26] The way in which we answer the question, "What do you think of the Christ?" that is, the *historic Christ*, will also determine our whole attitude to the Bible.

[25] From this viewpoint I cannot refrain from appraising the development of criticism as a divine dispensation for the church. Of course this appraisal is based on other considerations as well. For me it is connected with trust in God's educative rule over the church. For only in the light of that rule do the undeniable aberrations—those tending to orthodoxism as well as those ending in rationalistic naturalism—become comprehensible to me, namely, in that they mutually correct each other. If it is possible to discern the purposes served by such developments in the past, then we can and should assume the same to be true in our present situation, even though we are not yet in a position to see it in perspective. Such a perspective, which would reveal clearly our own limitations, would paralyze our working capacity, which, in accordance with our human nature, has a certain one-sidedness.

[26] Fr. Nippold, *Handbuch der neuesten Kirchengeschichte*, III, 2 (3rd rev. ed.; Hamburg: Gräfe und Sillem, 1896), 122.

INDEX

INDEX

Albertz, M., 34
Althaus, Paul, 3
Analogy, 25, 52-55
Apostles, 15, 18-19, 24, 44, 106-07
Arnold, Robert, 87
Authority; see Bible, authority of

Baillie, Donald, 35
Barth, Karl, 1-2, 8, 14, 33, 36
Bartsch, Hans-Werner, 3
Baur, Ferdinand C., 2, 5-6, 49, 54, 101
Beck, Johann T., 6, 112
Bengel, Johann A., 13
Bertram, G., 34
Beyschlag, Willibald, 9, 26, 62, 67, 74, 80, 102, 111, 121
Bible
   authority of Bible, 17, 31, 61, 87, 103, 110, 116, 119, 123, 129, 131, 135-39, 143-44
   canon, 110, 116-17, 123-24, 140
   inerrancy, 17, 28, 114-15
   infallibility, 111, 141, 147
   verbal inspiration, 2, 6, 17-18, 31, 108, 113-18, 125, 127, 140
   see also Word of God
Biblicism, 2, 28, 108
Biography of Jesus, 19, 22, 25, 34, 46-51, 55-56, 62, 70, 80, 82, 85, 93, 95, 103, 121, 127
Bornkamm, Günther, 37
Brunner, Emil, 33, 36
Bultmann, Rudolf, 1-3, 15, 21, 32-37

Carylye, Thomas, 79, 85
Christ
   biblical, 10-12, 14-15, 17, 28-30, 32, 38, 44, 65, 76, 86, 104, 119, 122-23, 126, 128
   dogmatic, 19, 43-44, 126
   historic, 10-11, 13, 15, 17, 21, 29, 43, 63, 65, 86, 91, 117, 119, 121-22, 148
   living, 19, 29-30, 42-43, 60, 91
   person and work, 60, 65-66, 80, 86, 95
   picture of Christ, 19, 22-23, 26, 47, 57, 62, 69, 72, 77-80, 84, 87-88, 91, 95, 97, 102-03, 120
   preached Christ, 19, 30, 62, 66
Christology, 2, 24-25, 56, 95, 102, 121
Cremer, Hermann, 129
Criticism
   biblical, 6, 17, 146
   historical, 10, 17, 26; see also historical research; historical science
   literary, 50, 101, 107-08, 141
   negative, 6, 22, 36, 48, 109
   positive, 6, 22, 48, 117
   see also Form Criticism

Dante, 124
Deism, 115
Demythologizing, 2, 37
Dialectical theology, 2, 35-37
Dibelius, Martin, 34
Dieckhoff, A. W., 110

150

INDEX

Disselhof, Julius, 113
Dogma, 24, 26, 68, 72-73, 77, 83-84, 95, 121
Dogmatics, 13, 44, 47, 56, 62, 67-69, 102
Dogmatism, 26, 43, 46, 148
Dorner, I. A., 44, 46, 53

Ellwein, Eduard, 3
Enlightenment, 8, 12, 42
Epistles, 44, 82-84
Erasmus, 115
Erlangen school, 2, 8, 14
Existentialist theology, 20, 38
Ewald, P., 49

Faith
    authoritarian, 26, 72, 74, 110
    basis of faith, 9-11, 14, 16, 28-32, 36
    content of faith, 10, 13-15, 29, 32, 74
    definition of faith, 17
    productivity of faith, 11, 14
    see also Justification through faith
Fascher, Erich, 33-34
Form Criticism, 2, 24, 33-34, 36, 38
Fourth Gospel, 34, 44, 49-50, 78, 81-82, 84, 89-90, 108
Francke, A. H., 108
Frank, F. H. R. von, 8
Fuller, Reginald, 21

Gerhardt, Paul, 4
German Idealism, 4
Gess, W., 82
Godet, Frédéric, 101
Goethe, 4-5, 52
Gospels, 19-24, 34, 44-45, 48-52, 55, 59-60, 68, 80, 82, 84, 93, 126-28
Gotthelf, Jeremias, 52

Hamann, Johann G., 42, 113
Harnack, Adolf von, 24, 117
Harnack, Theodosius, 61
Harvey, Van A., 38
Haupt, E., 49, 59
Hegel, G. F. W., 44

Hendry, George, 35
Hengstenberg, E. W., 17, 109
Herrmann, Wilhelm, 9, 11, 14-16, 30, 32, 58, 77, 84, 119, 129
Hess, Johann J., 62
Heussi, Karl, 81
Historical research, 20, 26, 47, 54, 57, 62, 74, 92, 95, 109-14, 121, 145
Historical science, 14, 27, 30, 61, 107, 119-20, 139
Historicism, 16, 18, 22, 26, 28, 43
Hoffmann, Heinrich, 75
Hofmann, J. C. K. von, 2, 7-8, 11, 13-16, 116-17
Holtzmann, H. J., 101
Hundeshagen, K. B., 104

Jesus
    divinity of Jesus Christ, 14, 25, 103-04
    historical Jesus, 10, 14, 18-21, 32, 36-37, 43-44, 47, 65-66, 84, 120
    humanity of Jesus, 18-19, 25, 46, 50, 58, 103
    inner life of Jesus, 14-16, 52
    "Life of Jesus," 5, 24, 48, 56, 68-69, 73, 125, 127
    "Life of Jesus" movement, 1, 18-19, 22, 24, 36, 43, 46, 57, 147
    messianic consciousness, 15, 50, 80, 103
    sinlessness of Jesus, 25, 53-55, 79, 85, 103
    uniqueness of Jesus, 25, 46, 53-59, 70, 79
    words of Jesus, 59, 82, 85, 88, 94, 106
    see also Biography of Jesus
    see also Christ; Christology
    see also Resurrection
Jewish theology, 64
Judaism, 54, 108, 115
Justification through faith, 6-9, 17-18, 28

Kähler, Anna, 5
Kähler, Ernst, 7, 33
Käsemann, Ernst, 37

151

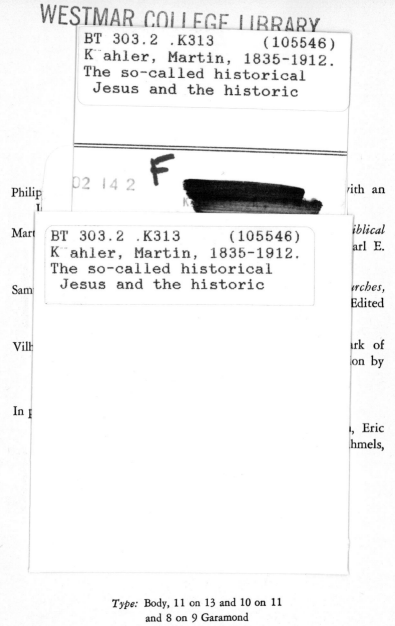

Type: Body, 11 on 13 and 10 on 11
and 8 on 9 Garamond
Display, Garamond
Paper: 'R' Antique